THE REAL GENESIS
HIDDEN IN
PLAIN SIGHT

Creation, Extraterrestrials, and the
Defense of Adam and Eve

Mel Martinez, Esq.

Copyright © 2022 by Mel Martinez, Esq.
Edited by Laurie Knight

The Real Genesis Hidden in Plain Sight
Creation, Extraterrestrials, and the Defense of Adam and Eve

All rights reserved.
No part of this work may be used or reproduced, transmitted, stored or used in any form or by any means graphic, electronic, or mechanical, including but not limited to photocopying, recording, scanning, digitizing, taping, Web distribution, information networks or information storage and retrieval systems, or in any manner whatsoever without prior written permission from the publisher.

The Holy Bible Self Pronouncing Edition © 1968 by The World Publishing Company. Used by Permission. All Rights Reserved Worldwide.

An Imprint for GracePoint Publishing (www.GracePointPublishing.com)

GracePoint Matrix, LLC
624 S. Cascade Ave
Suite 201
Colorado Springs, CO 80903
www.GracePointMatrix.com
Email: Admin@GracePointMatrix.com
SAN # 991-6032

An application to register this book for cataloging has been submitted to the Library of Congress.

ISBN-13: (Paperback) – 978-1-955272-16-2
eISBN: (eBook) - 978-1-951694-89-0

Books may be purchased for educational, business, or sales promotional use. For bulk order requests and price schedule contact:
Orders@GracePointPublishing.com

CONTENTS

Introduction vii

Chapter 1	In The Beginning	1
Chapter 2	The Tradition	8
Chapter 3	Telltale Signs	.12
Chapter 4	All Alone Without Any Help	.18
Chapter 5	Manifest Illogic or That Does Not Compute . . .	.21
Chapter 6	The Big Picture	27
Chapter 7	Theological Pretzels	34
Chapter 8	Round Pegs & Square Holes	39
Chapter 9	God-Creator's Mercy	.41
Chapter 10	Describing the Indescribable	44
Chapter 11	Creation—The Play of Opposites	48
Chapter 12	The Synthesis	54
Chapter 13	Conclusion	57

Note From The Author 63
For Further Reference 65
About the Author 67

INTRODUCTION

WE'RE ALL FAMILIAR WITH THE story of Adam and Eve in the Bible's book of Genesis. God created the heavens, the earth, and the beautiful Garden of Eden where He placed His creation of the first Man and Woman, Adam and Eve. The story tells how they disobeyed Him by committing the first sin, thus called the "Original Sin," by eating the fruit of the Tree of the Knowledge of Good and Evil. That sin therefore entered the world and would plague all mankind with punishment for all time and finally death. God then cast Adam and Eve out of the Garden to live hard and difficult lives for their one transgression.

That's the surface story we know and which has been handed down to us from one generation to the next for thousands of years. But what if there is a deeper spiritual and metaphysical meaning with a more profound message hidden inside the same account? This may sound rudimentary, but allow me to digress briefly for the sake of clarification. By "spiritual" and "metaphysical" I'm simply referring to things that are not physical, that don't have a physical body or presence. "Meta" means beyond, hence metaphysical simply means beyond the physical. It could be like a thought, feeling, perception, an internal knowing, an "ah hah" moment when something suddenly becomes clearly understood.

Sometimes important messages are presented to us with different levels of meaning which can be understood differently depending on the person's depth of awareness and capacity for understanding spiritual and metaphysical matters. The first level is the plain meaning of the words. Then there is a deeper meaning which can be extracted because of the person's particular knowledge or similar life experience. Then there is a deeper meaning still simply because the person just knows it to be true without being able to clearly explain it in words. It's a knowing beyond words and beyond logical explanation. It's like spirit talking to spirit or truth recognizing truth. It just is. This is within the human experience. Sometimes you just know. Most likely we've heard a man or woman say, "He's the one" or "She's the one" followed by "I just know it."

Such is the creation account in Genesis particularly with regard to Adam and Eve. Although the account has been taken as literally true for thousands of years and been the linchpin explaining why all mankind must suffer during life and finally endure death, that's only the obvious surface meaning. Spirit is telling us there is more to this story than meets the eye. We just know it. A deeper meaning recognizes that there are enough indications, even in the literal account, that it was not meant to be taken literally and should not be! Rather, there is a deeper meaning within the story revealing to us the nature of God and the very meaning of creation which was so awesome that two accounts were needed—one for the universe and us as humans and one for other sentient beings with awareness that we might call extraterrestrials.

As I write this, I feel that I have to tell you that I do so only with reservation. I am like a reluctant muse who has been put into a position where I must act and go forward. I am not one to seek the limelight. Admittedly, I am more of a "behind the scenes" type of person. However, I have been pushed, pulled, and bashed on the head to get moving on this so I have finally given in. Even as a child I naturally gravitated toward the spiritual and metaphysical. As I grew older, the affinity for such things only grew. I was always fond of saying that people should be aware of how the Divine touches their life. It starts gently, perhaps with an idea like a gentle breeze across your cheek. If you don't take heed, the contact will be stronger, like a shove on the shoulder. If you still don't respond, you may get hit with a brick on the head to gain your attention.

I have received strong feelings and indications that I should write my ideas down about this matter for some time now. I then started to write some things. Then I would get what I'm sure are more messages to continue. For example, a family member would be watching a program on TV that I could see from the other room, and suddenly bold print would come across the screen whether it was an advertisement for a product or part of the show: WRITE, WRITE, WRITE! I couldn't help but feel that message was meant for me.

One weekend afternoon I was channel surfing and suddenly I saw Deepak Chopra on public television giving one of his presentations which lasts several hours. I tuned in just exactly at the perfect time when he was telling the audience that if they had a question about what they should be doing, they should simply listen to the feeling or ideas coming from within themselves. I immediately knew for me that meant to write!

Late one day after work I went to the YMCA for a workout. While walking from the car to the entrance, I was thinking about some metaphysical stuff. Four steps inside the building I suddenly felt and heard a blow to my head and I blacked out for an instant. I didn't fall down; I was able to remain standing. When I came to, I shook my head, looked around, and asked the attendant at the front desk if she saw what happened. She didn't see anything. I looked around and saw a metal object on the floor. It was a metal Christmas angel but there were no rafters or flat surfaces above from where it could have fallen. Also, it was well past the Christmas season. I reasoned that nobody could have thrown it because they would have had to throw it from a greater distance, forcing it to hit me with much greater impact than it did. In short, nobody was able to determine how it could have happened. There was blood on my head and I filled out an accident report. I was able to do my workout but my head did hurt. I had headaches for a couple of weeks but then they went away. To my way of thinking, that incident was the brick on the head that I have often mentioned to others when God is trying to get someone's attention.

As you can surmise, He definitely has my attention now. Being desirous of avoiding escalating incidents of physical trauma but also wanting to let my muse out, I now put forth my best efforts at writing on this subject matter.

To be fair I must state at the outset that I humbly approach this topic, not as a theologian, pastor, or biblical scholar, but rather as a practicing Catholic and student of Scriptures with a college level minor in theology and philosophy from a Jesuit university. I also address this topic as an attorney with a rich experience and background defending clients in criminal cases, crafting complicated estate and business plans which must comport with various legal, investment, and IRS requirements, and in helping clients resolve serious disputes without the need for scorch and burn litigation. My desire is not to lock horns with the theological and academia establishments. However, my background and experience have fostered in me an objective and critical thinking approach to beliefs and reasons. My perception and understanding of this subject matter come from totally different disciplines and experiences. This is what I now share with you. As I do so, I humbly state that I am only the messenger. I readily acknowledge that the ideas and statements in this manuscript come through me but not from me. I invite you to make your own assessment of them.

I readily acknowledge that many sincerely believe that the Bible is the infallible word of God and should be understood and accepted literally. However, even those adherents must recognize that there are many different versions of the Bible and many different translations as well. There are about 50 main versions of the English Bible in circulation to say nothing of the many versions in several different languages! Also, the Catholic, Jewish, and Protestant faiths have their own Bibles.

The many different Bibles don't all say the same thing in every instance nor do they have the same books or even the same number of books. For example, the Catholic Bible has 73 books and the Protestant Bible only 66.

In addition, the different Bibles are updated in different ways to reflect changes in the meanings of language and new discoveries such as the Dead Sea Scrolls which gave insight into life and beliefs of the time. For example, the Biblical instruction that you are to pluck out your eye or cut off your hand if they cause you to sin was preached as a literal admonition. However, it was later realized that exaggeration and hyperbole were used by ancient scriveners as shock and awe techniques to call attention to and emphasize a particular point. The real meaning here was to change one's heart and mind for the better which would cause the needed change in thoughts, beliefs, and actions. Another example is that consuming Christ's body and blood shockingly sounded like a form of cannibalism to Western thought and way of thinking. However, to the Eastern mind it clearly meant one must completely accept and live one's life in accordance with His teachings such that, in your own way, you become more and more like Him.

Thus, even those who believe the Bible to be the infallible word of God must recognize that a certain amount of flexibility must be accorded to the Divine to keep His love relevant and meaningful to current and future generations. In other words, the Creator obviously put us on a path for continued growth and understanding of the Divine because we simply cannot fathom and understand it all in one gulp but only little by little. He provides helpers along the way to reveal, bit by bit, the awesome treasures which have been hidden for future generations to discover when they're ready to accept an expansion of awareness. How the Diving chooses to reveal this is completely up to Him.

In this regard I am reminded of the Old Testament Book of Numbers account (11:25-29) where an Elder tried to convince Moses to stop "unofficial" elders from prophesying to the people even though God's spirit had rested on them also. Moses immediately recognized the jealousy and asserted his desire that the Lord would bestow His spirit on everyone, not just a few!

A similar incident is reported in the New Testament (Mark 9:38-40) where John tells Jesus that they saw someone driving out demons in Jesus's name and they tried to prevent him because he was not one of the disciples. Jesus responds abruptly that they should not prevent him because he is clearly a friend and not an enemy.

Thus, sometimes there's a tendency to make matters of the Divine an exclusive club limited to certain professions or impressive titles. However, no one controls how and when the Divine chooses to act. That's an arrogant attitude which has no place in such matters. The Divine recruits in a variety of ways including through inspiration which can be accepted and acted upon or not. For my part, I can only answer the call and go where I am led.

You may think of it as a journey to a place you've been before many times. Instead of taking the same highway you've always taken, this time you're going to take an exit off- ramp and drive on smaller back roads and country roads to arrive at the same destination. You won't be driving as fast as you would on the highway, but you'll be taking in a lot more scenery and appreciate the drive a lot more. Unlike the highway, you can stop on the side of the road, get out of the car and breathe in the fresh air, smell the flowers, and even take pictures of the small streams and brooks-things you never noticed before while whizzing by on the super highway.

On this slower journey you'll delve deeper into the text and be able to appreciate the genius of Genesis and how it spoke to ancient cultures and later generations by deftly using symbolism and a type of code, or what I call Godspeak. Thus, cultures of the day could understand the plain meaning of the words, yet later cultures, enlightened by experience and wisdom, could grasp the deeper meanings and messages hidden therein. Thus, in only a few lines of text and a couple of chapters, Genesis encompassed the whole of creation, presaged extraterrestrials, and dealt with the emergence of sin and evil. Let the journey begin!

CHAPTER 1

IN THE BEGINNING

IMAGINE, IF YOU WILL, WHAT it must have been like before there was a beginning, before there was creation, when there was only God—no place, no venue, no up, down, or sideways, no hot, cold, or lukewarm, and no water, land, earth, sun, solar system, or cosmos, just God. We can't even imagine what that would look like or be like.

Then imagine, if you will, that God isn't going solo anymore. There won't *just* be God. Rather, there will be God plus whatever He creates. Whatever He creates will be an "extension" of Him in some way, a part of Him in whatever way He decides. In other words, God will relate and have a relationship in some way, with whatever He creates. Whatever He creates will relate back to Him and have a relationship with Him, in some way. At a specific point in "God-time," God will experience Himself through His creation. Thus, in a way we can understand, creation means relationship.

Basically, the creation account is telling us that creation is about relationship. Creation IS relationship. Thus, Creation=Relationship. All creation is in relationship with itself and with everything else that is created. Thus, it is telling us of God's relationship with Himself and His creation. It is also telling us of the relationship of the creation with itself.

Since creation means relationship, there must also be a morality or code of conduct which applies to everything that is created.

With regard to God's relationship with His creation, the following logically and necessarily flow and are part and parcel to that creation:

> First, there is God's relationship with Himself. In the creation account in Genesis 1:26, God says, "Let *us* make man in *our* image, after *our* likeness." God is like members (plural) of a family (singular). It seems like a precursor to the much later concept of the Trinity, three persons in one God. The "God Family" may be the model for His other creations including the human family.
>
> Second, there is God's relationship with the inanimate world and the plant and animal world.
>
> Third, there is God's relationship with Adam and Eve (humans), sentient beings with awareness described in the second creation account (Genesis, Chapter 2).
>
> Fourth, there is God's relationship with other men (male and female), made in His image, also sentient beings with awareness, described in the first creation account (Genesis, Chapter 1), different from Adam and Eve described in the second creation account (Genesis, Chapter 2).

With regard to the relationship of creation with itself, the following logically and necessarily flow, and are part and parcel to that creation:

> First, is the relationship between Adam and Eve with each other, a couple—the beginning of a human family modeled after the "God Family."
>
> Second, is the relationship between man (humans) and the physical environment.

Third, is the relationship between "man" and "man" i.e., between the two sets of sentient beings with awareness (Genesis, Chapter 1 & 2), humans and what we might call "other men." In the creation account, God first creates "man in our image, after our likeness… male and female he created them" before He creates Adam and Eve in the second creation account.

Old Testament commentators try to explain that the first creation account of "man, male and female," *before* the creation of Adam and Eve, really refers to Adam and Eve. However, nowhere else in the account does God create something and then repeat doing it again a second time as if He forgot the first creation. Furthermore, the account's first creation of "man" is not specific as to how it was done. God just "created man in his own image." However, the creation of Adam and Eve are specifically described as unique creations separate and different from anything else that was created, even the first creation account of "man." God formed Adam from the dust of the earth and breathed into his nostrils and later put him into a deep sleep whereupon He formed Eve from one of Adam's ribs. Clearly, Adam and Eve are intended as different creations, separate and apart from the earlier creation of "man" in the first creation account. Thus, there are two distinct creations of "man."

The first creation account, the creation of "man" before the creation of Adam and Eve, could refer to other beings, other humans, or non-humans, or even what we might call in today's language, extraterrestrials (ETs). The original descriptions in the creation accounts would not know what else to call them or how to refer to them other than to say that God did create them, and they also are made in His image. The author(s) wouldn't have the science or cosmological understanding to actually call them "extraterrestrials," "greys," or something else. Therefore, simply calling that separate creation "man" would be a logical and likely thing to do.

Lest you think these are the only creations of "men" mentioned in the creation account I would point out that later on, Cain, the first child of Adam and Eve, kills Abel, their second child. God therefore exiles him to wander in the land of Nod, east of Eden. Because Cain is an outcast, he fears that others may find him and slay him. God tells him, "Not so" because He will put a sign on Cain letting others know that if they kill him,

God will take vengeance on them "seven-fold." There is no explanation as to who these other potential killers are or where they came from or even whether they were human, non-human, or whether they were even made by God or some other creator. Obviously, they are not progeny of Adam and Eve.

Thus, taken as a whole, it seems reasonable to surmise that the creation account was trying to forecast and tell us that we (humans) will be in relation with these other "men" who are also God's creation of other sentient beings with awareness made in His image. It had to be hidden in the original written account because no one would know what else to call them, what it meant, or to what or whom it referred. The very concept of other beings, human or otherwise, perhaps inhabiting other worlds in the cosmos would not and could not have been understood at the time.

The core message, originally concealed in hidden language, is being revealed and is clearer to us now because we are ready or will be ready both for the contact with these other "men" soon and to be in relationship with them. Our attitude should be that it was foretold as far back as Genesis and it is coming to fruition now because we are fast approaching the time when we will be ready for such relationships.

As a matter of fact, there is a growing belief that there are other beings, so-called extraterrestrials, in the vast cosmos that have visited earth long ago. Zecharia Sitchen, an Azerbaijani-born American, dedicated his adult life to the study of such matters. He authored several books on the subject and proposed that human origins involved contact with what we would call extraterrestrials. He attributed the ancient Sumerian culture to such contact.

Furthermore, the very idea of such extraterrestrial contact on Earth in ancient times is growing worldwide as evidenced by such topics gaining a foothold in news reports and social media. The popular television program, *Ancient Aliens*, on the History channel enjoys a growing international audience, and similar programs now take the form of documentaries with credible input from professional historians, researchers, scientists, archeologists, theologians, and other reputable and learned people.

Much of the world's adult population was practically raised on weekly episodes and full-length movies of *Star Trek, the Next Generation* and the voyages of the *Starship Enterprise* whose purpose was to "boldly go where no man has gone before." Many young viewers became lifelong fans and entered professions dealing with science, technology, astronomy, space travel, and the like as a result of the extraordinary impact the series had on their imagination. Its creator, Gene Roddenberry, was the genius behind the magic. In addition to being wildly talented, he had unique access to NASA and the space exploration industry. The character names of Captain James T. Kirk, Spock, Bones, Uhura, Scotty, Sulu, Chekov, and Captain Jean-Luc Picard entered the daily vernacular in languages worldwide. The actors, William Shatner, Leonard Nimoy, DeForest Kelley, George Takei, Patrick Stewart, and many others became household names. Although it was clearly fiction, Gene Roddenberry insisted that the episodes present as fiction with a purpose and a serious underlying message. The audience was treated to a variety of future real-life situations between humans from earth and many different intelligent beings with awareness from several different star systems. Themes dealt with peace, battles, war, and always the morality of a given action or non-action. As they traveled through the cosmos and encountered civilizations on other planets, the "Prime Directive" was to take no action which would interfere with or influence that civilization; it would have to proceed on its own. The inhabitants had to make their own choices and decisions. As a result of the massive influence of *Star Trek*, much of the societal culture has been conditioned for decades, ready to accept the idea of beings on other worlds, and that we will have contact with them, forming relationships.

In that vein we must mention Erich Von Däniken, the illustrious author of the sensationally popular book, *Chariots of the Gods?* published in 1968. The Swiss hotel manager must have written this treatise in his spare time. While attending to his managerial duties, a part of his mind was undoubtedly racing ahead with big ideas about the cosmos. In this regard he reminds us of Albert Einstein whose ideas about the cosmos, energy, and relativity were nurtured while he was employed in the Swiss patent office. (There must be something very special in the Swiss water to produce such innovators!)

Similar to my own background, Erich Von Däniken has Catholic roots and was educated by the Jesuits. He began his journey into the cosmic realm by asking questions. His Catholic school education taught him that God dwells in the perfect place, Heaven. But he was also taught that Satan began his great rebellion against God there. He then questioned how that was even possible. How could there be a battle of angels in Heaven, the perfect place where God was? To him, it didn't make sense. This greatly troubled him and he asked his teachers about it. One of the Jesuit priests directed him to the book of Enoch which did not make it into the Bible but it answered his immediate questions and a whole lot more. Thus did his real journey begin.

He posed many questions in his own mind, then set about to answer them by his own research and many travels. Similar to Zecharia Sitchen, he concluded that early man was helped by visitors from outer space who imparted advanced knowledge of the cosmos, mathematics, and geometry. These so-called Ancient Aliens were ultimately responsible for the many pyramids and massive structures with precise cosmic orientations found all over the world.

At first the professional communities laughed at him and ridiculed him for such nonsense. However, the notoriety attracted more and more onlookers and observers turning them into serious investigators themselves. In the end, the naysayers had no explanation how primitive groups with rudimentary tools could be responsible for erecting colossal structures with critical orientation and alignment with the earth and far away constellations. Obviously, they couldn't do it by themselves. They needed extraordinary help, and the doubters were forced to at least consider Erich von Däniken's ideas. He employed the scientific method by asking questions, doing the research, travelling to many sites throughout the world, and following the evidence which led him to the stars.

In addition, bear in mind that much, if not most, of the world population from the beginning of time has believed in other beings who are in other places. Everybody who prays or has ever prayed to or for a departed loved one, saint, angel, or deity accepts that they are "in being" in some other place—a spirit world which some call heaven or some other name. Perhaps without realizing it, they are expressing a belief in *other-dimensional or extra-dimensional beings,* and they have no problem with that. Many spiritual and metaphysical writers, including the great Emmet Fox, have stated that there are worlds within worlds within worlds. Even science accepts that there are many different dimensions and that beings in one dimension could be in our world, but we would not be able to see them or even be aware of them because their nature is ethereal, and their movements are much faster than we could even measure. In comparison, our dimension is heavy and slow.

Thus, if great numbers of people already believe in and are obviously comfortable with other-dimensional beings, accepting the idea of other physical beings in our world and our same dimension would be comparatively easy.

What follows is an analysis of the account of Adam and Eve, its literal explanation, and the deeper meaning hidden within which contains no less than a Divine invitation into a more profound relationship with God-Creator. It is also a foretelling of future relationships with His other creations, including "other men," i.e., sentient beings with awareness whether they are humans, non-humans, or what we might call extraterrestrials.

It is well to bear in mind that the first two chapters of Genesis deal with all of creation including the two creation accounts of "man" which covers some 13.8 billion of our years. Also note that Genesis does not give any indication of the time between the separate creation acts of the Creator. Although many take the Bible literally, the reference to "days" in Genesis is a form of poetic license, not scientific fact. Thus, the first reference to the creation of "man" could have taken place hundreds, thousands, millions, or even billions of years before the second creation of "man." We just don't know.

I bring that up at this time because if it is part of our destiny to eventually be in relationship with these other "men," how we relate to them will depend on how close we are to each other technologically, mentally, and even spiritually. If we are hundreds of years apart is one thing. However, if we are millions of years apart, that is quite something else. In either case, the contact may initiate a rapid evolution of our species far beyond anything we have been able to imagine.

CHAPTER 2

THE TRADITION

THE NAMES ADAM AND EVE have become easily recognizable, echoing across the ages of all mankind throughout the world and among all cultures and faiths including atheists and agnostics. In effect, the whole of mankind has heard of them, and everyone knows to whom it refers whether or not they believe the Bible.

Simply by pure acclamation, the "Adam," in Adam and Eve, has become the most maligned man in all of history, probably even eclipsing Pontius Pilate in terms of sheer name recognition for bad acts. That's really saying something especially considering the fact that the name Pontius Pilate is mentioned in every Mass every day throughout the world and spoken through the lips of the millions of people in attendance at those Masses!

The massive name recognition of Adam is boiled down to a single act. As far as we know, it's the only act he ever did! Most people are gauged by their body of work over an extended period of time or even a lifetime. However, in Adam's case we don't know much of anything else he ever did of any significance.

We really don't know much about him. We don't know what he looked like. Was he tall or short? Was he muscular or skinny? How many push-ups could he do? How fast could he run around the Garden of Eden and what was his time to do it? Was it improving with the passing of time, or did it stay the same? What kind of women was he attracted to? Did he prefer blondes or brunettes? What kind of a lover was he? Since the Garden of Eden was perfect and everything in it was perfect, Adam must have been perfect too. He therefore must have been able to do the perfect number of push-ups and run around the Garden of Eden in perfect time. And, of course, he must have been the perfect lover.

Adam's one act is said to have frustrated God's intent for mankind to no end and is responsible for all the misery in the world and the entire so-called human condition. Who was this man who looms so large in impacting human history? He is hardly mentioned in the Book of Genesis in the Bible. He doesn't really stand out like a giant personage of historical magnitude, yet he has reportedly had more impact than all the Caesars of the Roman Empire, Genghis Khan, Alexander the Great, Hitler, Churchill, all the kings and despots of the world, all the presidents, or any other human luminary across the ages.

According to the biblical account, for some unexplained reason, Adam's one act frustrating God's original intent necessitated a completely different result for all mankind; that different result is our history and our future. It is described as salvation history or salvific history which is God's way of saving mankind from the effects of the evil act of Adam. Incidentally, and as an aside, there is no indication in the biblical account what would have happened if only Eve had transgressed and not Adam. Biblical scholars address this and I believe it can be stated that they generally conclude that Eve's transgression alone would not have resulted in ruining God's original plan for mankind. As another aside, many conclude that Eve's possibility of being the only transgressor leads many to conclude that the Adam and Eve account is simply an allegory, not a description of something that actually happened with a real first man and woman. Many spiritual and metaphysical writers, including Emmet Fox, have opined that it is clearly an allegory where Eve represents the emotional nature of both men and women, and Adam represents their logical nature. That Eve succumbed to the temptation first means that our emotional nature gets us into trouble first and our logical nature follows that lead. For example, when we are wronged, our emotional nature responds immediately with anger and soon thereafter our logical nature kicks in plotting ways to get even. However, for purposes of this work, I will proceed, taking the biblical account at face value.

Have you ever thought what would have happened if Adam and Eve did not eat of the forbidden fruit? There wouldn't be a story or a Scripture because there wouldn't be much to say. Everything would be perfect, and everyone would get along with everyone else. There would be no accidents, earthquakes, floods, or even bad weather. There would be no pain, suffering, sorrow, illness, disease, or death. With no deaths, the ever-increasing population would have to be dealt with by an increasing land mass, the earth would expand to accommodate it or something else would have to happen.

Also, consider that without Adam's one act, there would be no need for salvation history and therefore no:

Jesus, Son of God	Last Supper	Religious
Holy Ghost (Spirit)	Easter	7 Sacraments
Pentecost	Resurrection	Parishes
Catholic Church	Apostles	Martyrs
Muslims	St. Joseph	Collection Baskets
Hindis	Mary, Mother of God	Saints
Sin	Popes/Cardinals	CYO
Jewish Faith	Priests/Bishops	Religious Education
Christmas	Nuns	Rosary
Passion & Death of Jesus	Brothers	Christian Churches

Neither would there be any battles, wars, bombs, tanks, warships, nuclear missiles, or nuclear warheads. In effect, there would be no long history of men and women fighting each other for status, land, power, or riches.

You get the idea.

Adam is maligned but his one act in a single moment in time basically formed the basis of our history, culture, and society itself. With such a profound and far-reaching result for all mankind through all ages, we must legitimately inquire as to what exactly was the evil act of the first man and woman that caused and created all the negatives of the human condition—pain, suffering, loneliness, poverty, disease, disappointment, and death.

Even Scriptural scholars and theologians readily admit that the Scriptures are not a scientific treatise. However, there are many who feel comfortable believing everything literally such as God creating the world in six twenty-four-hour periods and then resting on the seventh day. However, not everyone is satisfied with such explanations. There are just too many "hanging chads" and dead ends which demand and cry out for more believable explanations. After all, God did give us inquiring minds so we shouldn't be expected to have to check our ingrained search for truth at the door; if we had done that before, we'd still be thinking that earth was the center of the universe!

CHAPTER 3

TELLTALE SIGNS

THERE ARE CERTAIN TELLTALE SIGNS, both stylistic and substantive which indicate that the Adam and Eve account is not to be taken literally. Rather, it is a "tale," not fact—although an important tale with profound messages deep within but not obvious to the casual observer.

Stylistic Signs

The Adam and Eve account reads and sounds like a dream, a vision, or even like a Jesus parable which would begin with a story like, "There once was a landowner who owned a vineyard…" or "A father had two sons…" Jesus wasn't referring to a specific landowner by name or a specific father by name who had two sons. Rather, they are literary tools designed to set the table for a deeper truth or spiritual message. Similarly, we can conclude that there really wasn't a specific man and woman named Adam and Eve who disobeyed God for the first time ever which caused all the sorrow, hardships, and death for all mankind. Rather, the underlying message is this: God-Creator gave men and women the inherent power to create "good" and "evil" and they can choose between them. However, they must be aware that there are very negative consequences to creating "evil."

The creation account begins by setting the stage with beautiful sights and sounds of the magnificent creation of everything—the heavens, the entire cosmos, the earth, water, and all kinds of plants and animals. The Garden of Eden is beautiful and magnificent beyond words. What a perfect place for the very first young couple, Adam and Eve, to enjoy their honeymoon! Of course, God saw that everything He created was "good" and basically perfect.

Notice how everything is even beyond perfect. There are no dinosaurs, carnivores, and the animals don't hunt each other for food. There are no bad storms, and the temperature doesn't get too hot or too cold. Clearly, the setting is just too perfect, so the stage is set to ruin this idyllic scene. All this beauty and perfection is just too good to be true. It has to be interrupted or stopped completely or there is no story. Without some kind of interruption, everybody lives happily ever after in complete boredom and that's the end of the story.

The upset of this idyllic scene is "The Test." God tells Adam that he can enjoy everything in the magnificent Garden of Eden, but he is not to eat the fruit of the Tree of the Knowledge of Good and Evil. You can almost hear ominous music playing!

Then God creates Eve who will be a suitable companion for Adam. God delights in the first couple and goes on walks with them in the Garden. Throughout, it is understood that Eve is apprised of the prohibition regarding the Tree of the Knowledge of Good and Evil.

Then enter the villain—a completely loathsome figure, Satan, in the form of a *talking* serpent! How utterly nonsensical and fantastic at the same time! More ominous music plays! Rarer than a unicorn and another surefire indication that this is not a real occurrence, but rather an incredible make-believe story with a message. Of course, Satan targets the woman with his advanced trickery and through her, Adam falls.

Notice how the woman is the real culprit here. If it weren't for her, Adam would never have sinned and all mankind wouldn't be in the predicament it's in. Of course this reflects the very patriarchal and societal belief of many ancient cultures that women are manipulative, evil seducers who are responsible for bringing good men to their ruin. If you believe the Adam and Eve account is of divine origin and infallible, then you must conclude that God harbors the same type of prejudice against one of His own creations!

When God discovers the fall, He becomes enraged like the ancient despots and the gods of mythology thereby unleashing a complete overkill punishment, not only against the new couple, as ancient tyrants and mythical gods would do, but also against all their progeny extending into the distant future for all time. Surely this God was equally badass and then some of any of the sordid tyrants and gods of old. This God would not be outdone in cruelty when compared to those lesser gods and tyrants.

Then there is the further indignity of being thrown out of the Garden of Eden. And, of course, God had to take some measures to make sure they didn't sneak back into the Garden unawares! So, He posts a Cherubim angel at the entrance to make sure that didn't happen.

To add to the "shock and awe" of the situation, the angel standing guard at the entrance has a "flaming sword" to make even more sure that Adam and Eve didn't try to sneak back in. Thus, if they tried to regain entrance, not only would they risk being run through with a sword (which would be bad enough, since it was a *flaming* sword), but they would be burned as well as impaled! A double whammy! No doubt seeing the "flaming" part at a great distance would discourage Adam and Eve from even attempting to get too close to the entrance.

Just the image of an angel standing guard at the entrance with a flaming sword forces one to silently wonder where that angel was when Satan entered the Garden as a talking serpent. Adam and Eve could have really used that angel's services then!

Also, one has to wonder how that particular angel was chosen for guard duty that fateful day. It is said that Cherubim are pretty high up in the angel hierarchy even to be in God's presence constantly. Guarding the entrance to Eden would be pretty lonely duty, like being an army of one with no one to talk to or visit with during the slow times. Realistically speaking, it would all be slow times with nothing really to do! It doesn't seem that it would be a promotion or reward for good angel works. On the contrary, looking at it objectively, it seems pulling that guard duty would be considered more of a punishment for some sort of angel bad acts.

So that's the tale—truly a picturesque scene conjured up within only few lines of content, yet filled with everything you could want to form a truly indelible mosaic in the mind, easily remembered by young or old: resplendent beauty, young love, heaven on earth, a honeymoon, a Greek tragedy before there was a Greece, hell on earth, punishment without end even for billions who weren't there and hadn't even been born, and a cruel form of engendering fear and mind control over a scared, largely uneducated, and compliant population.

Substantive Signs

The account of the first sin, so-called "Original Sin," purportedly sets the stage for the need for salvation history and therefore warrants a healthy scrutiny. In the account, God changes from being the perfect, all-powerful Creator to an anthropomorphic god just like gods of pagan cultures and mythology. God suddenly takes on human characteristics and traits and as such, He can be offended by lesser beings, even his own creations. And if offended, just like the gods of mythology, He can exact vengeance against the culprits to show them who's in charge.

He befriends his man-woman creations and even goes on walks with them and talks with them in the Garden of Eden. However, the closeness and friendship apparently ends rather quickly. He sets up a test for the new couple to find out if they will obey him. Just like the historical models of any other despotic king of antiquity, he demands absolute obedience from his subjects and is capable of exacting draconian punishment for the least failure. He tells Adam he can have anything in the magnificent Garden except for the fruit of the Tree in the middle of the Garden. Afterwards God creates Eve and the account intimates that she was also aware of the prohibition. Then without any explanation, Satan suddenly appears on the scene described as a talking serpent and the most cunning animal that God had made. How did Satan enter and why was he suddenly there? Did God allow him entry? Did God know he was there? Did God *invite* him in? There's no explanation for any of this, yet we are expected to swallow this whole and not ask any questions? Really?

Satan engages Eve in conversation and convinces her to eat the forbidden fruit which she shares with Adam, hence the fall. As a result of this "Original Sin," death entered the world where before there was no death. Adam and Eve would now have to die. Things would not come easily to them anymore. Now they would have to work by the sweat of their brow and oftentimes be disappointed by their results and efforts.

Throughout the account, it's as if God puts on different masks and then acts them out. First, He's the perfect creator, then He becomes like a mean tyrant. He's not the unchangeable, immutable creator who creates out of love and loves His creation. It's as if He creates just so He can punish. If that's the case, wouldn't it be better not to create anyone at all?

In the account, Adam and Eve are told to be fruitful and multiply. But they only had two sons, no daughters, and one son killed the other son. How were they supposed to propagate their species and populate the world with those numbers? Even if they did have daughters wouldn't their children have to join together with each other? Apparently, incest was not a problem in the early stages of humanity.

The creation of other "men" or extraterrestrials in the Adam and Eve account creates a thorn in the side of "Original Sin." Does the taint of Original Sin apply to ETs or not? If so, exactly how does that work? Do extraterrestrials have the capacity to sin? Can they commit venial sins, mortal sins, and sacrileges? Do they have souls? Where do their souls go when they die, if they die? Do they have their own versions of the Adam and Eve account? Does our salvation history with Jesus incarnating, suffering, and dying on earth apply to them too or does Jesus or some other savior incarnate in their world and suffer and die for them? What if they came on the scene eons before Adam and Eve? What if they were not put to a test?

My theology professor, who was a practicing theologian, taught us about a then-cutting-edge concept of the Cosmic Christ. Jesus would travel to other worlds throughout the whole cosmos saving those worlds as He had saved our world. The concept had not yet defined how the saving act would take place and whether it involved incarnating, suffering, and dying as in our world or whether the act performed once in our world sufficed for all worlds in the whole cosmos. And of course, there is the question as to whether those other beings on other worlds even need saving.

As an aside, it is interesting to note that Pope Francis has publicly stated that such beings are not subject to the effects of our so-called "Original Sin." He has also stated that he would accept extraterrestrials into the Catholic Church. While that may seem to be a generous offer, from another perspective it could be considered quite provincial. After all, why would advanced beings from another world light years away want to join a church on our planet? Would such beings even have a concept of "church" as we understand it? Conversely, if there are churches on other worlds light years away, would we want to join them?

As you can see, these are rather imponderable ideas with no clear answers. However, if there is no "Original Sin" as traditionally described, and no real first couple who committed it in our world, then the problems posed by the existence of extraterrestrials goes away. Our salvation history stays intact even without a fall by Adam and Eve because just in living life, all have sinned and need God's mercy and love which are manifested abundantly every day and especially in Jesus.

Apart from those reasons, I would simply ask whether it seems just a bit bizarre and unhealthy to blame all of our problems, shortcomings, and the whole human condition on the single transgression of an ancient ancestor, supposedly the first of our species, committed eons ago under the strangest of circumstances. And that one act is said to have frustrated an All-Powerful God to the point where He had to initiate a Plan B. Really? If you posit an All-Powerful, All-Knowing God, how can He be forced in an underling's (Satan) plan? Who's really in charge? It seems we were only left with bits and pieces of the truth and now we really need and are ready for the rest of the story.

CHAPTER 4

ALL ALONE WITHOUT ANY HELP

AS A RESULT OF THE "fall," sin also is said to have entered the world with seemingly inexhaustible expressions of misery and even multiplying in complexity as the world marches onward. "Original Sin" has multiplied itself exponentially into virtually infinite variations of problems. We might ask how something bad in the beginning could morph itself into virtually infinite expressions of evil going forward.

What is a reasonable explanation as to how the "Original Sin" could morph into virtually infinite expressions of "bad" things? Strangely, it's as if the Original Sin itself had the internal, almost infinite power going forward to make more "bad." Do we dare say or even think that the God-Creator imbued that Original Sin with such a negative, almost infinite force going forward? Who or what else had the power to imbue that first sin with virtually infinite staying power to multiply itself exponentially, each iteration becoming more "God-Awful" than the previous one?

If the answer is the God-Creator, then you've got the untenable problem of His being the very source of all that is "evil." However, if you posit that there was some other source, then you've got the problem of some other creator like a Negative God-Creator.

Although it sounds preposterous, the latter at least explains how God-Creator's plans are always being thwarted by some other evil "force." As the account goes, the God-Creator's plan was for humans to live in complete love and perfection in the Garden of Eden perhaps forever. However, some other force, Satan, frustrated that original divine intent, hence we have the world with all its problems. And, of course, let's not forget Heaven when the God-Creator created the angels. How well did that turn out? The God-Creator's original intent was thwarted again by some evil force.

And what about tests? The Adam and Eve creation account reveals that very soon after creating them, God gave them a test. Without any explanation or warning to them, God is said to have allowed a prior creation that went really bad (Satan), to use clever, diabolical trickery to get them to go against Him. Thus, at that moment, sin is said to have entered the world.

So, as the account goes, God allowed the most powerful and ungodly being to be unleashed on little Adam and Eve without any warning or prior instruction on how to deal with it – no defenses, no countermeasures, and no diversion tactics. There were no warnings, not even advice, and not a single class. Does that really sound like a loving Father? In this encounter, who was on the side of Adam and Eve? Anybody or anything? According to the account, God wasn't even on their side!

I recently heard on Catholic Radio that "Adam and Eve just blew it. They could have had a wonderful experience and us too but they just blew it." Of course, this reflects the traditional Church teaching. But truly, doesn't that sound rather harsh? After all, this was the first temptation on planet earth as far as we know and Adam and Eve had to face it alone, without any help, not even from God! They literally didn't even have a prayer because there literally were no prayers! They couldn't go to anyone else for help or advice because there was nobody else. They couldn't go to God because He wasn't their friend in this matter. According to the account, He set up the trap with his newfound friend, Satan. Even if they had gone to God for some help, He wouldn't be able to help them. He would have to recuse Himself because He had an interest in the outcome!

Compare and contrast their situation with any human being faced with temptation. We all have hundreds if not thousands of prayers we can use for any situation, and we can even make some up if we want! Furthermore, we can go to God (who will be on our side), Jesus, the Holy

Ghost, St. Michael the Archangel, Raphael, our own guardian angel, Mary (Mother of God) St. Joseph, plus more than 10,000 saints recognized by the Church. Of course, Adam and Eve had none of that.

In the Heavenly Garden of Eden where everything was perfect, where God Himself is said to have walked and talked friendly-like with His creation, where there was no such thing as evil, God is said to have allowed the unleashing of the most diabolical evil in that magnificently beautiful place against a naïve, innocent, and unsuspecting first couple to get them to fail with all the unimaginably bad ensuing consequences for themselves and all of mankind yet to be.

CHAPTER 5

MANIFEST ILLOGIC OR THAT DOES NOT COMPUTE

REALLY? WASN'T THE OUTCOME PRETTY well determined beforehand? Wouldn't that be kind of like a modern battleship going up against a mere life raft? Without some help, Adam and Eve didn't stand a chance against the king of deceit, Satan. The end result of that encounter was a foregone conclusion.

One might logically ask why the All-Good Father did not warn and better prepare his creation for the diabolical onslaught and deceit that was about to happen. Furthermore, what father would engage and even conspire with the enemy, the devil itself, to tempt and bring down His newly created children? According to the account, God set up the trap by allowing Satan entry into the Garden with the specific purpose of attacking the naïve couple. What father would allow or permit the devil to go after his new creation? Furthermore, wouldn't an All-Knowing, All-Powerful God know the results of a foregone conclusion anyway?

God's human creation had no knowledge, understanding, or comprehension of evil. They would have been woefully unprepared for the encounter. Nor did they have the benefit of learning things through childhood, adolescence, and adulthood. They were supposedly perfect beings in a perfect place, created by the perfect creator, God Himself. How could they even remotely comprehend the concept of deceit and evil, much less the nadir point of such evil? Isn't this the most extreme example of an overindulgent parent whose children live in a bubble and have not been prepared for the real world? Finally discovering what God's real world was like must have been a real shock to the first couple when the demonic deceit had been suddenly thrown at them. Do you think the first couple felt anger and resentment toward God for not being up-front with them about what His world was really like and hiding the truth which lulled them into weakness thus assuring the fall?

So why, it might be asked, would the perfect Heavenly Father set up and orchestrate this diabolical encounter in the first place with certain failure for the first couple? Does that really make sense after what we are told of the Loving Father who only wanted to share His happiness?

We are taught that, after the "Original Sin" God's plan of salvation for all mankind had been planned out from all eternity, i.e., even before creation. Obviously, this is meant to convey God's love for all mankind, but doesn't it also convey something else? If it was planned from all eternity, didn't He know Adam and Eve would fall? But what if Adam and Eve hadn't fallen because of the test? Would God have given them another test, and another one, and another one ad infinitum until He had the fall He was looking for and wanted? Were Adam and Eve basically set up so there would be a Fall no matter how long it took or how many tries were required?

The account we have been given is obviously inconsistent and problematic even considering our very limited understanding of things divine. Our very being cries out that something is missing in the account and/or the account itself is not accurate and is leading us incorrectly. We really need the rest of the story!

According to the account, Adam and Eve could have anything in the Garden, except for the fruit of one tree in the middle of the Garden. Eve is then engaged in conversation by Satan who lies to her saying that if they did eat of that fruit, they would become equal to God and they would know what is good and what is evil.

Adam and Eve must have known they were the created beings and that God was their creator. They also knew that God had created everything around them in the magnificent Garden—the plants, animals, water, beautiful sky, and so forth. Surely, they knew and understood that they could not create these things. No way! So, by merely eating the fruit of that tree they were going to suddenly become creators equal to the God that created them? Really? Nobody, not even Adam and Eve, could have believed that. Nobody could really be so naïve and stupid!

The account continues. That one act of "disobedience" was so bad, so frighteningly terrible, that evil suddenly engulfed Adam and Eve in the most negative way and their progeny forever through all generations in an instant. The evil which was somehow created that day grew and expanded in countless ways like a cancer infecting every aspect of human life and relationships for all time. The act was so awful, heinous, and offensive to God that He would exact punishment from all their progeny forever and ever. The description of God suddenly changes.

As stated previously, God suddenly became an anthropomorphic being who gets angry and vengeful against His recent creation who did Him wrong. From an All-Good, Beautiful, and Wonderful Being, He becomes just like the other gods of the pagan world—treacherous, merciless, vengeful, and demanding sacrifice as a way to make amends for the awful act that was done to Him. Such gods of antiquity demanded burnt offerings or sacrifices of plants, then animals, and then human to make amends for the "wrongful acts" of humans that were supposedly done to them.

Those gods would have their appeasement and, according to this account, this God was no different. This account would call for human sacrifice too but since this was the real God, just plain human sacrifice would not do. It would have to be a perfect sacrifice because the perfect God was offended. Only God could be the perfect sacrifice so a "part" of the perfect God would become human and offer Himself to Himself. It would be to make amends for the single bad act of the first man and woman and later include all bad acts of their progeny.

Notions of bad acts or "sins" by humans and appeasements by sacrifices to the gods were held by virtually all cultures throughout the world. Anthropomorphic gods were said, by the priests of virtually all cultures, to have demanded sacrifices for all sorts of supposed human wrongs.

But what exactly was the actual offense of the first couple that was so bad and utterly terrible as to destroy their magnificently wonderful experience in the Garden of Eden and condemn all of mankind for all generations to suffer and endure all kinds of negative experiences including physical and emotional pain, disease, grief, loneliness, sadness, and death? Was it some horrible crime which could be listed in a penal code or even the Ten Commandments punishable by life imprisonment or death? No! It was a simple case of a child disobeying a parent over a trivial matter. What child hasn't done that and what parent hasn't experienced that?

I'm sure some will say it wasn't a trivial matter to which the response would be this: If it was such an important matter why wasn't it communicated as such? On the scale of venial sin and mortal sin, where would it register? Exactly how was the All-Powerful God hurt, damaged, or somehow diminished by it? Exactly how was all of God's creation thereby rendered a nullity because of it thus requiring an alternate world of unimaginable negativity to replace it? "Because God says so and He makes all the rules" will be their cry. But doesn't that completely belie the very nature of the All-Good, All-Knowing God-Creator who only wants to share His happiness? Somehow punishing a distant great-great-great-grandchild for a single transgression of the matriarch/patriarch committed eons before doesn't seem right or fair under any measure you choose.

This is not to challenge or undermine Scripture. We were all taught, and we all accepted this traditional account. However, in our present state of consciousness we cannot help but ask questions and posit that there must be another explanation. Not to criticize the Scriptural authors, but something *must* have been left out. There must be a different explanation, a more complete explanation which addresses our naturally inquiring minds which are not satisfied by the explanations handed down from centuries ago. On closer scrutiny, they don't ring true and they don't match up. Perhaps those thumbnail explanations satisfied a largely uneducated populace that could be more easily controlled, but today's inquiring minds want and need much more, especially when that meager explanation is supposed to explain and justify the many lifelong trials of the human condition where no one is immune.

Punishing Adam and Eve and all their progeny for all time because of the so-called "Original Sin" may be termed *Atonement Theology*. This concept took hold in theological circles and which the Church embraced with a vice-like grip since the eleventh century when it was promulgated by St. Anselm, the Archbishop of Canterbury. His *Satisfaction Theory of Atonement* went like this: God was offended by "Original Sin" and all human sin and was somehow diminished by them. To be made whole, He required satisfaction or payback otherwise there would be no forgiveness. In legal parlance, "satisfaction" is the fulfillment or payment of an obligation by one party (Adam and Eve and all mankind) which is due to the other party (God). Rather legalistic, wouldn't you say?

Why would God lay out any temptation towards evil to the newly created man and woman anyway? If God is All-Good, how could He even conceive of such a negative thing so utterly and completely the opposite of His own nature-being? Is it actually possible for an All-Good God to create evil and the functionality of evil? How could His creations, Adam and Eve, do evil if evil did not first exist in some way? How was it that sin entered the world anyway as a result of their transgression? Did their action actually create evil? If evil entered the world, wouldn't it have to already exist somewhere, created by someone or something else? Can we posit that evil did not create itself? It had to come from something else. What could it have been?

If God is omniscient, all-knowing, and beyond time, why would He need to test Adam and Eve anyway? Being omniscient, wouldn't He know the outcome of the test which He set up and established? A test is only needed to find out something you don't already know. Didn't God already know what would happen? Since He is beyond time, wasn't their future bad act already a completed act in God's time?

The Scripture is silent as to how Adam and Eve could have even had the ability to compare the two choices presented to them: Do what I tell you and you will have the good fortune to be able to continue enjoying all the wonderful things in this wonderful Garden, or disobey me and suffer the consequences that look like this—pain, suffering, disappointment, disease, all sorts of hardships the rest of your life, and finally death. Were they shown what would happen if they did eat of the forbidden fruit? Did God prick their finger with a pin so they could feel what a little pain felt like? Did they really have free will? How could they have really known what they were choosing?

What about the notions of fair play and that the punishment should fit the crime? Here, there was a single transgression by one man and one woman which caused untold misery and suffering for themselves and billions and billions of human beings yet to be born eons into the future until the end of time. Those future generations weren't guilty of an original transgression so why should they have to suffer? Where is the justice in that? How is that a loving expression of an All-Loving and Forgiving Father?

Furthermore, whatever happened to the notion of a Merciful God? Remember the Prodigal Son? Why did Adam and Eve only get one chance, only one bite at the apple, so to speak (no pun intended)? Surely, they would have done better the next time.

In like manner, whatever happened to second chances? Here, only one strike and you're out, along with all of mankind, who, by the way, never even got a first chance to choose. In effect, Adam and Eve chose for all mankind yet to be, without any input from those billions. Furthermore, they did not even know they were choosing for all those billions, which they would have no way of even imagining.

CHAPTER 6

THE BIG PICTURE

HERE IS A GOOD PLACE to review where we've been and to grab a peek at where we're going.

With so many obvious questions and issues just regarding this one topic, how, you might ask, were the literal explanations in the Bible taken as truth for thousands of years without question? Well, for one thing the Church was *not* tolerant of any other explanation and if you dared question or contradict Church teaching on the matter, you risked losing your head or being burned at the stake. The Bible was considered the oldest book in the world, written by God and therefore it was infallible.

You will recall the great Italian astronomer Galileo was severely sanctioned by the Catholic Church for his *heretical beliefs and teachings* that the sun was the center of our solar system and not the earth. The Inquisition tried him in 1633 and he was kept under house arrest until his death in 1642. He avoided being burned at the stake by publicly recanting his scientific findings. It wasn't until 1992 that the Vatican formally and publicly cleared him of any wrongdoing. Interestingly, Pope John Paul II said the theologians who condemned him did not recognize the formal distinction between the Bible and its interpretation. In speeches before the Pontifical Academy of Sciences and in other public statements, the Pontiff stated that this led the theologians to unduly transpose in the realm of the doctrine of the faith, a question which in fact pertained and belonged to scientific investigation. The condemning Church had incorrectly applied Psalms 93:1, 96:10, and 1 Chronicles 16:30 text stating that, "the world is firmly established, it cannot be moved." Also, in Psalm 104:5, "the LORD set the earth on its foundations; it can never be moved." Also, in Ecclesiastes 1:5, "And the sun rises and sets and returns to its place."

In the nineteenth century, universities and museums funded expeditions to Mesopotamia with the purpose of finding physical evidence which would validate the biblical accounts as stated. However, the expeditions discovered something quite different. They found written cuneiform tablets with narratives which appeared in the biblical accounts but actually predated them. It was as if the biblical versions lifted out older Sumerian texts which had been reduced to writing long before. For example, the Sumerian Flood Story predated similar flood stories in *The Epic of Gilgamesh* and the Noah's Ark story in the Bible.

The cuneiform method of writing was developed in the valleys of the Tigris and Euphrates rivers which became known as Mesopotamia. I still remember my theology professor, the theologian, telling his class that it was believed that the Garden of Eden was most probably in the "Fertile Crescent" between those two rivers which would be present-day Iraq. At the time I remember thinking that it shouldn't be hard to find. Just look for a really beautiful garden between those two rivers. Then I researched it and I discovered that the topography in that area had changed over the centuries and much of the land was now under water. To the dismay of many, none of the expeditions found any evidence of Adam and Eve nor of any first couple. As an aside, neither did they find any evidence of an angel's sword, flaming or not!

However, the discoveries they did make spurred further investigations all over the world and led to the discoveries of incredible civilizations that had achieved advanced knowledge of the cosmos, planets, and the movement of heavenly bodies. Magnificent buildings, pyramids, and edifices found all over the world revealed that very old civilizations had advance knowledge of mathematics, geometry, construction methods, and the ability to move and position massive stones and align them with constellations without the benefit of modern-day mega-moving machines.

Many observers and researchers concluded that these ancient civilizations had the benefit of help from other worldly beings to accomplish these incredible feats. As previously mentioned, Zecharia Sitchin and many others pioneered this research particularly in the ancient Sumerian culture and concluded that human origins involved the help from a race of extraterrestrials from another planet. Many researchers and professionals who have seriously studied this subject worldwide have arrived at the same conclusion. The rudimentary tools and building methods of ancient cultures simply could not have been wholly responsible for the enormous pyramids, temples, and other structures found all over the world.

It used to be thought that pyramids were only in Egypt, but then pyramids were discovered all over the world. Although their outer forms differed according to their locale, their basic structure, building methodology, and even the placement of the stones and building materials seem remarkably similar. Furthermore, their alignment with certain constellations in the cosmos are eerily related if not substantively identical. It's as if they all used the same blueprints from one master architect and builder. Positioning massive stone structures so sunlight enters a small opening at sunrise on a certain day, year after year (e.g., summer or winter solstice), cannot be luck or an accident. Even a slight angle or degree off would render the whole massive structure meaningless. Such precise measuring and placement reveal advanced knowledge of mathematics, geometry, and astronomy. Obviously, this level of sophistication greatly exceeded the capacities of the early civilizations where these structures have been discovered.

It seems that the more science studies such matters additional factors are discovered. For example, looking at the physical position of the pyramids around the world from space reveals what could be described as a web similar to a geographic power grid. There is an intriguing alignment of ancient sites with pyramids or massive constructions forming a great circle around the earth: Angor Wat in Cambodia, Mohenjo Daro in Pakistan, Giza in Egypt, Nasca in Peru, and Easter Island in Polynesia. Also, the Great Pyramid of Giza in Egypt is aligned to true north and apparently has a mathematical relation to the speed of light. One of its geographic coordinates is 29.9792458° N and the speed of light is 299,792,458 meters per second. If they are coincidences, they are of astronomical proportions. Literally!

The search for extraterrestrial life has gone mainstream. Many scientists who work in this field now state that the detection of extraterrestrial life is a question of when, not if. For example, in 1977, NASA, with the help from astronomer Dr. Carl Sagan of Cornell University, sent an interstellar message on two Voyager spacecrafts in the form of a golden phonograph record containing sights, sounds, music, and diagrams of humans and the position of our earthly home in the cosmos. Of course, it was directed to extraterrestrials in space. Both spacecrafts are still travelling in space at a speed of 35,000 miles per hour and they, in effect, represent humanity.

In the desert near Albuquerque, New Mexico, the Very Large Array (VLA) Radio Telescope consisting of twenty-seven large radio antennas points skyward as if standing at attention before the cosmos. Its purpose is to search for radio waves which would reveal the existence of intelligent life in the universe. Each antenna is twenty-five meters (eighty-two feet) in diameter and weighs 230 tons.

The Search for Extraterrestrial Intelligence (SETI) Institute, known worldwide, seeks to answer the question, "Are We Alone?" It states that the number of potentially habitable planets in our galaxy alone is close to one hundred billion.

Dr. Steven Greer left his profession in medicine to become a ufologist full time and founded the Center for the Study of Extraterrestrial Intelligence. He has studied and researched the UFO phenomenon, written about his findings, and made documentaries about this subject which are seen on mainstream platforms such as Netflix. He has filmed many live interviews with responsible individuals from all walks of life including high ranking government officials, scientists, researchers, and those involved in space exploration. His work reveals the many types of contacts people have experienced with UFOs and extraterrestrials.

Daniel Sheehan is a constitutional and public interest lawyer who has worked in many high-profile public interest cases. He has a keen interest in the UFO phenomenon and alien visitation, and advocates for much more disclosure about these topics. He has even stated publicly that he wants to meet with extraterrestrials. He speaks on these subjects and offers animated interviews about them on Gaia, which is an international alternative media service, and on relevant documentaries broadcast on streaming services such as Amazon. His unique background and experience as legal counsel for the Jesuit Order of the Catholic Church make him one of the few people with access to the Vatican's evolving understanding of extraterrestrials.

Although many of the world's institutions have not evolved in their understanding or acceptance of the extraterrestrial phenomena, we are accelerating towards a cosmic destiny, which was foretold long ago, whether we feel ready or not.

Looking back on this journey, it's truly remarkable how we have arrived here talking about extraterrestrials. It began with the very old belief that the Bible was the oldest book in the world, of divine origin, and that it must therefore be infallible. Expeditions were sent to Mesopotamia in the nineteenth century with the specific purpose of gathering physical evidence validating the biblical accounts, but they discovered a lot of other things leading to the focus on other worlds and extraterrestrials. From the big picture at 35,000 feet, we get a better view of what is happening to us on our planet.

Themes of extraterrestrial contact in the entertainment industry have been growing in popularity for decades and the population has become more accepting of them. Examples are several *Star Trek* episodes for television with different sets of actors, several *Star Trek* motion pictures, *Stars Wars, Stargate, 2001: A Space Odyssey, Independence Day, Arrival, E.T. The Extra-Terrestrial*, and *War of the Worlds* just to name a few of the more popular or recognizable titles. The internet and its power of instant communication everywhere with computers and cell phones has become an accepted reality on the planet. UFO sightings and even contacts with them have been reported and investigated worldwide with increased frequency. Mutual UFO Network (MUFON) is currently the oldest and largest UFO network in the world. It investigates and reports on all types of UFO contacts and maintains the information in a computerized case management system with over 100,000 cases. It has chapters in all fifty states and over forty-three countries. Furthermore, it maintains a nationwide rapid response team for high value investigations and a trained underwater dive team. These folks are serious and are proof that this phenomenon is real. Bear in mind that this is not the only group either; there are others throughout the world. In addition, most countries maintain their own UFO reporting systems which include civilian as well as military protocols.

The timing of these events could not be an accident or merely fortuitous. Viewing them objectively, we could conclude that they are converging together with purpose and a plan which will bring big changes to our world. Spiritually and metaphysically speaking, our world has been moving rapidly toward a new age of enlightenment. It may not seem that way on the surface or from the news reports, but it is. Spiritualists and metaphysicians say it has been moving in that direction for some time but now it is accelerating. The movement is towards a future where many of the old things and institutions will go away and new ones will replace them. It's all positive and there is an unseen Hand guiding all of this. However, we must be aware that this type of massive change will have opposition because many entrenched business and economic interests will go by the wayside or disappear completely as they will no longer be needed. As a world society, we will make this change and it will all be positive. A big part of the change will include more contact and communication with extraterrestrials which will actually help our relations with each other on our own planet earth. The constant wars and mistrust among peoples and nations have to stop and this coming change will help.

Many scientists and futurists estimate that we are about one-hundred years behind where we could be in terms of science and technology. For example, we have known for a long time that there is tremendous energy potential in a simple glass of water which could be harnessed to produce enough free energy to run large machinery and even provide power to cities. However, there are huge problems getting it to market because so many powerful entrenched forces don't want the change because it would threaten their economic interests. They fear the specter of free energy for everybody, everywhere. In spite of that, change is coming, and it will not be stopped. Many scientists and researchers think that extraterrestrials may be thousands or even millions of years ahead of us in terms of science and technology. Our contact with them may be able to help propel us on a new road of discovery including better ways to harness the energy which is all around us and create a new level of medicine where diseases can be cured and even prevented much more effectively than we can now.

Far from being something to be concerned about, our contact with extraterrestrials can be understood and accepted as part of the plan of creation where Creation=Relationship. Thus, it was foretold long ago that we will be in relationship with them, and that time is quickly arriving.

In one sense, perhaps we will be meeting ourselves, i.e., our ancestors who already subdued the earth and had dominion over it. Bear in mind that in the first creation account of "man… male and female" (Genesis, Chapter 1; i.e., not Adam and Eve), God gave them the injunction to be fruitful and multiply and to subdue the earth and have dominion over it. Perhaps they already did that and have gone on to other worlds in the cosmos to subdue and have dominion over them as well and are still doing it. As the first creation of *man*, perhaps they were the beginning of another "race" not part of the so-called "Original Sin" of Adam and Eve with no need of salvation. In a sense, meeting them would be like coming home again.

CHAPTER 7

THEOLOGICAL PRETZELS

TO TRY TO MAKE THE account of Adam and Eve fit into the straight jacket of a very narrow dogma, theologians twist themselves into weird-shaped pretzels trying to justify the guilt and punishment of all succeeding generations of humans who had nothing to do with the so-called "Original Sin." According to them, all succeeding generations who really didn't have anything to do with the "Original Sin," will still be held guilty anyway just as if they had been there acting with Adam and Eve. Incredibly, that sounds a lot like the IRS tenet of "putative income" where a taxpayer never actually receives the income, but the IRS concludes that, as far as they are concerned, the taxpayer did receive the income and will be taxed on it anyway just as if the taxpayer really did receive it. It's a game of make-believe. This version could be labeled "putative guilt." We can understand and perhaps expect such an IRS tactic, but why would that be part of the essence of God and Church doctrine?

"Putative guilt" is also like a guilt-by-association argument. It's much easier to hold somebody guilty of something just because the person is somehow associated with a malefactor instead of having to actually prove that the person committed a bad act. Here, theologians basically make a guilt-by-association argument by throwing all of humanity into the same pot as Adam and Eve (i.e., since we are human, we share in their guilt just as if we had eaten the forbidden fruit). Although such arguments formed part of the history of our criminal law, guilt by association is no longer a valid argument, and is not permitted. If even we, in all our imperfections, can eliminate that injustice, why would it still be held as a major tenet of Scriptural belief and theological teaching?

Recently I heard a radio commentator say that we aren't being punished for their sin, but because of it. Adam and Eve became different beings, apparently several notches below where they were before the sin. Because of their sin they had become different, flawed, and tainted beings and because we are their progeny, we inherit their demoted theological status. Because of them we are also flawed and tainted and therefore must live difficult lives full of problems, disappointments, loneliness, and finally death. We are now forbidden to enjoy the beautiful life like that in the Garden of Eden. What a theoretical, pretzel-twisted explanation! How is that *not* punishing us for what they did eons ago? That explanation creates an end result which is the same just as if we ourselves had committed the sin in the Garden.

We have been taught that the sin of Adam and Eve was so bad and that God was so offended that a sacrifice had to be made to God to put things right, to make up for the horrible affront to God. As noted above, this was part of St. Anselm's Atonement Theology. Note that this sounds identical to the sacrificial demands by pagan gods of all ancient cultures. When humans offended the gods, the gods demanded sacrifice. Thus, slaying of animals and burning of crops was done in sacrifice to appease these gods. When the offense was particularly grave, the priests of many cultures said that the offended gods *demanded* human sacrifice. Hence beautiful and pure maidens and young men were killed in rituals of human sacrifice to appease the gods.

Because of the extreme gravity of the offense, the sacrifice ultimately required would have to be human sacrifice. But humans were tainted due to putative guilt assessed against all men and women because of Adam and Eve. Therefore, the sacrifice had to be a perfect sacrifice because a perfect God had been offended. Since there obviously were no perfect humans, a God-Man had to do it. Therefore, God sent a part of Himself to earth to be the perfect sacrifice, Jesus Christ. Eons after the "Original Sin" the

God-Man came to earth and, through a most strange series of events, He is beaten and nailed to a cross where He dies and the perfect human sacrifice was complete. It is said that this saving act of human sacrifice atoned for "Original Sin" and the sins of all men and women and was planned by God from all eternity, thus even before creation.

A few questions arise from the foregoing. If the saving act was accepted by God as setting all things right after the "Original Sin," then why does all of mankind still have to suffer under the human condition just as Adam and Eve did after being hurled out of the Garden of Eden—physical and mental pain, sorrow, loss, disease, disappointment, and death? If Christ's death on the cross conquered death, why do we still have to die? If the debt had been completely satisfied once and for all by the sacrifice of the God-Man, why was all humanity not immediately restored to the equivalent of the original Garden of Eden? Is there still some aspect of the original trespass against God that is not fully atoned for yet? Will that lingering lack continue for all eternity? If the God-Man, Jesus Christ, through His horrible suffering and death, could not completely wipe away the original trespass and affront to God, what could?

We must also bear in mind that sacrifice in the Jewish tradition was mainly done out of thanksgiving to God, not for expiation of sin. Thus, a farmer would offer ten percent of his yield to God in thanksgiving for the good harvest. If someone committed a sin, he/she could bring a sin offering as a step to getting right with God, but not so that God would be placated, made whole, and then be merciful. God's mercy always came first. God didn't need to be made whole first by an offering from the person. So-called Atonement Theology may not like this but a sacrifice is not required for God's mercy. Rather, God's mercy comes first and if He wants, He can demonstrate that mercy in any way He wants, even by assuming human nature then suffering and dying.

Did Adam and Eve really have the capacity to make a conscious choice in the Garden? All they had known was "perfect"—a perfect God and a perfect place, the Garden of Eden in all its splendor, where everything was just as it was supposed to be and everything worked as it was supposed to work. Thus, there was no comparison ahead of time for them. There was no setting up "perfect" on one side and "not perfect" on the other side so they could see what things would look like if they ate the forbidden fruit. They didn't have the benefit of a side-by-side comparison. They couldn't compare perfection on one side and not perfection on the other side with its misery, pain, suffering, loneliness, and death. If they had had that opportunity, how could they ever have chosen the "not perfect" side? In our not-so-perfect world, even hardened criminals know ahead of time the direct results of committing a crime or not committing it. No such warning or explanation was presented to Adam and Eve.

Have you noticed that, in the creation account, Adam and Eve are portrayed as a fully adult man and woman contemporaneous with Old Testament or New Testament times and possibly college-educated? They are certainly not portrayed as apes, cavemen, or Cro-Magnon specimens. As far as we know, they were not born to human parents. As the account goes, they are the first parents, so they are the Originals. So, they were apparently created into fully adult form without having gone through infancy, childhood, adolescence, young adulthood, or even much adulthood. Accordingly, they did not have much human experience. Neither did they have much couple experience with each other or with anyone else for that matter.

For them, there was no learning from their mistakes because there were no mistakes. As soon as they were created, everything that God had already created was already perfect, so they had no way of comparing good, bad, or indifferent. There was no "bad," no grey area of "not perfect" but not "bad" either. There was only "perfect." Nothing was negative. Everything was always clear and as it should be.

There was no morality, no so-called "right" and "wrong" because everything was "perfect." Everything was just as it should be. There was no need for "wiggle room" or grey area because everything was just perfect, as it was. There was no need for comparisons because everything was already perfect just as it was.

Adam and Eve really had no basis on which to compare anything. As far as the creation account goes, they had no basis, no understanding about how to compare anything with anything else. They really couldn't even have conceived of telling God that this Garden sure is nice, but the grass really looks greener over there on the other side. Neither could they have conceived of telling God "This shade tree is really nice, but couldn't you make it bigger?"

Neither did they have the capacity to evaluate, compare and contrast, or to even arrive at logical conclusions. There was no need for that because

God had already concluded that everything He created was "Good." And if God Himself concluded that it was "Good," who could argue with that? Certainly not Adam and Eve who were enjoying it all. They had no reason to question anything.

I suppose some will argue that Adam and Eve were not just regular human beings but rather "Super Beings" with much higher intelligence and the capacity to truly understand the decision they were making. After all, they walked and talked with God and therefore must have had the Beatific Vision or something akin to it thus enabling them to make decisions with complete understanding. Really? If they really enjoyed that heightened understanding and awareness, wouldn't they have been able to see through the inane argument Satan made?

Have you ever thought about conversations that Adam and Eve would have had with each other after being kicked out of the Garden? "Boy, things were sure a lot better back in the Garden. Everything was perfect. Now, here we are having to labor and toil just to make ends meet."

Do you think they ever blamed each other for "The Sin"? But for that very wrongful decision, "We would still be there enjoying ourselves to no end, without end. As it is, here we are, having to toil and suffer all of our lives and then we have to die." No human, man or woman, has ever had such an enormous regret. How is it possible that they did not commit suicide? Not even modern-day psychologists or psychiatrists, Freudian or otherwise, would be equipped to help them out of such depths of despair.

Adam and Eve shouldn't be blamed for "sinning" and thereby thrusting all of humanity into the human condition with all its negatives. They were simply unprepared and ill-equipped for the devastating one-sided encounter with the king of evil. The ill-preparation could not have been their fault. Following the account logically, it had to be God's fault. Wasn't He the Divine Coach who should have gotten his "team" ready and better prepared for the encounter? Isn't that what a good coach is supposed to do?

But how could God be at fault if He is perfect? The logic seems to run into a bit of a buzz saw. After all, who wants to hold God accountable for such sloppy and even non-existent preparation? Even if He did fail miserably in this regard, who could hold Him accountable? Himself? There is no court above God.

CHAPTER 8

ROUND PEGS & SQUARE HOLES

RIGHT ABOUT NOW DOUBTS BEGIN to creep in about the creation account. Looking at the details of trying to fit it all together is like pounding round pegs in square holes. On closer examination, the account starts to unravel and come apart. That's not to say it's all wrong. There may be some core elements which are accurate in some aspects but the overall connecting details don't bind it together, rather they pull it apart.

It is well to bear in mind that many scriptural accounts, including the creation account, are meant to convey a deeper truth. Sometimes interesting stories with colorful descriptions and settings set the stage and background for an important message which should be taken to heart. Elements of language and culture as well as ancient stories handed down from succeeding generations are used to convey important messages in colorful ways to attract attention. The wise person knows the difference between the essential message and the colorful tapestry that carries it. The wise person doesn't reject the essential core of the message just because the tapestry doesn't make sense or fit perfectly.

We are told throughout the Scriptures, Old and New Testament, of God's infinite capacity for forgiveness. The illustration of such mercy in the parable of the Prodigal Son comes to mind. Recently I heard a preacher on the radio talking about that very parable. He says that, when the Prodigal Son returned home after a profligate lifestyle, he had a prepared and rehearsed statement that he wanted to tell his father explaining how he had made very bad decisions. However, the father would have none of it. He didn't want to hear any explanations, excuses, or reasons why his son had left. The father had forgiven him and that's all that mattered. And most importantly, there was no meting out of a deserved punishment for the transgression. On the contrary, there was a joyful celebration!

The preacher continued: When God forgives, He doesn't put the transgression in a digitized computer file to be brought out as a needed reminder of your mistakes and past transgressions for the rest of your life. When God forgives, the mistakes, transgressions, and sins have been erased with BleachBit. They do not exist anymore.

What a wonderful thought and feeling to have that heavy burden of sin and guilt removed from your life forever—to be given a fresh start, a tabula rasa, to start over again. How wonderful is God-Creator! However, returning to the Adam and Eve account, God-Creator was not so forgiving of their apparent transgression. There were no second or third chances. One strike and you're out in the God-Creator's Garden.

And as for God not remembering a transgression ever again, well according to the doctrine of putative guilt, this God-Creator never forgets that original transgression, indelibly ascribed to all succeeding generations, and He even continues to bring it up at the conception and birth of every child even though none of them participated in it in any way. The God in the account of Adam and Eve is infinitely different from the God-Creator that we have come to know in the rest of Scripture.

CHAPTER 9

GOD-CREATOR'S MERCY

THROUGHOUT THE BIBLE WE ARE told of God's mercy which is boundless. The Jews didn't always follow God's word, but they were always welcomed back by the God-Creator who always forgave them. We recall the Genesis account of Abraham bargaining with God not to destroy Sodom and Gomorrah if only a few ever-declining number of righteous people could be found. The parable of the Prodigal Son powerfully recounts the father who forgives and welcomes back his wayward son without any punishment and restores him to his household as if he had never left. Let's not forget Jesus's words that there is more rejoicing in Heaven over one lost soul who returns than for the ninety-nine who remain constant and never stray. Also recall Jesus's response to Peter who asks how many times he must forgive. He asks if it was really seven times. Jesus's response is not just seven times but seventy times seven times!

Furthermore, Jesus's life taught people what His Father is like, i.e., boundless love and mercy. Jesus did not condemn or even insult the woman who was caught in adultery and was about to be stoned to death in accordance with the law. Jesus didn't punish her nor did He tell her that she would face some horrible torment and suffering for her continued adultery over many years. In John 8:11, He simply said, "I do not condemn you" and "Go and sin no more." Do you really think that Jesus had some secret, horrible punishment waiting for her which He failed to mention?

Neither did Jesus condemn the woman at the well who had five husbands, nor did He say that she would have to be punished. He never told anyone they would have to be punished before He would forgive them. Simply put, if they repented, they were forgiven, period!

So how do these clear accounts and teachings square with what could only be called the God-Creator's non-forgiveness of Adam and Eve? On the one hand we are told of God-Creator's boundless and never-ending mercy and that we are to forgive each other unceasingly. Yet God-Creator couldn't forgive Adam and Eve for their single misstep? Keep in mind that Adam and Eve really had no way of assessing the significance of the test or the consequences of their decision. They didn't even know what a test was. Furthermore, the account continues with what could only be described as God-Creator conspiring with Satan to assure their downfall. If that sounds inconsistent with our understanding of God-Creator, then something is obviously wrong. God is either forgiving and merciful or He's not. Otherwise, God-Creator is like those who say, "Do as I say, and not as I do!" That is, "You must forgive but I don't have to because I'm God!"

What about the concept of rehabilitation? In our own world the criminal law machinery has discovered that pure punishment without anything else leads to recidivism where the criminal keeps committing the same crime. Now we know that efforts at rehabilitation and job training help place the wrongdoer back into society and become a good citizen. It appears that those more humane concepts were clearly unknown, even by God, during the time of Adam and Eve.

Clearly something must be missing in the creation account that we have. Also, human beings are not perfect creations. We were made with inherent, built-in limitations of all sorts which must have been the intent and desire of the God-Creator. In the account, Adam and Eve had these limitations too and God-Creator knew that because He created them that way. Thus, creation is like a balance beam. On one side is mankind with all its faults, limitations, and problems. On the other side is God-Creator's mercy. Because humans are made with faults and limitations, there is the counter-balancing need and requirement for God-Creator to be forgiving and merciful. Thus, in a nutshell, the restated Adam and Eve account would say something like this: God created human beings flawed in lots of ways so issues would arise and there would be problems. However, the All-Merciful and Understanding God would forgive them and help them through the problems.

CHAPTER 10
DESCRIBING THE INDESCRIBABLE

SO, TO TAKE THE WHOLE creation account of Adam and Eve at face value, you'd have to believe that God was an ineffective coach who failed miserably in preparing His team for the competition and a cruel and unforgiving father who even conspired with the enemy (Satan) causing the downfall of His creation and their progeny for all time. Taken at face value, God is portrayed as even more conniving, treacherous, and evil than Satan! Of course, none of this could be further from the truth. Therefore, the true intent of the author(s) must have been to convey the idea that it is *not* to be taken literally but that there are deeper truths within it which are being communicated!

The creation account of Adam and Eve has been handed down for so long by so many in positions of influence and power, that most people have just accepted it whole, as it is, without much reflection or analysis. Thus, it has stayed in the Race Mind for thousands of years without much question. Of course, in metaphysical terms, the Race Mind refers to the group mind or group consciousness of humanity which includes limiting and negative beliefs.

This leads me to recall the writings of some "heavyweights" in matters of spirituality and metaphysics. Their explanations in the area go something like this: If God's whole creation was just so, perfect, with nothing challenging or bad, and no villain, well, that's just not much of a story. I remember being puzzled by that explanation wondering what it meant. If everyone got along with everyone else perfectly including God, and if everything got along with everything else perfectly, and there was no villain, what would be wrong with that? Wouldn't we all like that?

Wouldn't that be perfection, just like God? Of course, we assume that God gets along with Himself perfectly, so His creation would logically get along with itself perfectly too. And as far as it being not much of a story, well, to whom? What audience are we talking about? If we like conflict and problems, then no, it's not much of a story. But if the audience is God, then it must make a perfect story because everything is perfect and there is no need for a villain.

We must bear in mind that the nature of God is not like what we think. We only have a very limited capacity to understand the infinite nature of God. As humans we naturally think that God is like us. We tend to think that God thinks the same way we do. If we want something, we don't have it and that is why we want it. God doesn't want or lack anything because He already "has" everything, in fact He *is* everything. We also talk about God "deciding" to do something, taking some action, or "thinking" about doing something in the future as if He were subject to the limitations of time and space that we are. God doesn't need to weigh the pros and cons of doing something. It already has been done and always was done. Before "deciding" to do something, the moment immediately before is not empty and void of that "thought." In short, He is infinitely beyond our understanding and comprehension, but He does let us in a little bit.

In our very limited understanding of the Divine, we are inescapably led to the conclusion that creation itself must include opposites. So-called religious people, scriptural scholars, pastors, and the like are constantly saying that "God gave us free will" and that we have the power of choice. It's understood that it means we have the power to choose between good and evil. The obvious question which follows is this: Where did the two choices come from? Obviously, the "good" choice came from God-Creator. But what about the so-called "evil" choice? Where did it come from? Evil didn't create itself. It had to come from someone or something. God-Creator is the only creator as far as we know. Is it possible or even conceivable that the so-called "Evil" choice also came from the God-Creator or is that just too preposterous or sacrilegious?

If the God-Creator gave the angels and man "choice," didn't that choice have to come from Him? Doesn't that mean that the choice of "Good" and "Evil" came from Him? Is it so that the God-Creator gave the angels and humans the possibility of choosing "Good" or "Evil"? When you hear "God gave us free will" inherent in that statement is that God created the *possibility* for us to choose "Good" or "Evil."

If so-called "Evil" did not come from the God-Creator, where did it come from? If it came from some other source, then there is some other creator other than the God-Creator. It certainly complicates things to have a creator of "Good" and a different creator of "Evil." That sounds a lot like ancient mythology where a veritable stable of gods and goddesses had their particular areas of authority and control. Some were good and others were not good. These gods of mythology had relationships with each other and battled against each other. They also intervened in the affairs of men and women on earth helping them and hindering them as they saw fit.

If indeed that is the case, if there is a creator of good and a different creator of evil, then the biblical account and ancient mythology take similar tracks, at least in this regard of more than one creator. However, if that is not the case, how can we square an All-Good God-Creator with being the source of Evil? Perhaps it has something to do with our understanding of the nature of the God-Creator. We accept that God-Creator is "Good" and that what He creates is "Good." Could the notion of "Good" also include something that is not "Good" from our perspective but still be "Good" from the God-Creator's perspective?

To even talk about this, we have to conjure up what we think a God-Creator perspective could possibly be. But to continue, is it possible that what we call "Evil" is not at all perceived that way by the God-Creator? Is it possible that what we call "Evil" might be perceived as "Good" by the God-Creator?

Without trying to figure out the essence of the Divine or the actions of the God-Creator, we can only admit that full understanding for us is unattainable. At least we recognize that. It would be like trying to put Mount Everest into a small, pint size bottle. It just can't be done and there's wisdom in acknowledging that. So instead of trying to figure out all the aspects of God-Creator to our level of understanding, it would be more productive to limit our inquiry to only a single aspect. The aspect of most interest to us would be the aspect of creation itself and whether Evil emanates from that and why.

CHAPTER 11

CREATION—THE PLAY OF OPPOSITES

AS WE EXPERIENCE IT, AS we understand it, and as we observe it, creation itself and the act of creation is essentially the play of opposites. In some ways it can be described as the dance of opposites or the war of opposites. We experience it every day in our lives. The positive (+) and negative (-) charges enable us to have lights in our homes and offices, and to start our car in the morning, etc. In the world we know, both positive and negative are needed to make things go, to make things work.

Perhaps there are other worlds that are not based on the play of opposites, but we know nothing of them and cannot even imagine what they would be like. We are relegated to only begin to fathom the world we live in and our experience in that world. The play of opposites in our experience is how we live in all aspects of our life. This play of opposites is actually an insight, a brief look, at the essence of the God-Creator, or at least the aspect of the God-Creator that is being revealed to us. Of course, there may be other aspects which are not being revealed to us. But for our purposes, our world, and our experiences are bound up in the play of opposites.

Is it possible that the play of opposites, which is a reflection of the God-Creator that we perceive, has been incorrectly described in our history and culture? We are told that the God-Creator is All-Good and that Evil suddenly sprung from the nothingness because of some act of a created entity. In some way, which is beyond our current understanding, is it possible that what we call Evil may not be a separate "thing" as the opposite of Good, but rather the other "pole" of the God-Creator, i.e., part of God-Creator but being the negative (-) pole as opposed to the positive (+) pole?

I have always been troubled by the explanation that Evil suddenly sprang from the nothingness because Adam and Eve ate the fruit of the Tree of the Knowledge of Good and Evil. Note here that Adam and Eve could not have had an understanding of "Evil." Remember that they were in the Garden of Eden and walked and talked daily with God and had no understanding of anything other than "perfect."

Perhaps the writers of these accounts used "Evil" as a way of describing the opposite pole (-) in the creation process, the other pole of the God-Creator. If Evil suddenly sprang from the nothingness, how could that be? Who or what created "Evil" or the possibility of "Evil"? Who or what brought it into being as a possibility? Aren't we told that the God-Creator created everything? If something else created "Evil," then what or whom? If that is the case, then there has to be a different creator than the God-Creator we are talking about.

There is an apparent and obvious difficulty in describing something so unknowable as the Infinite, the God-Creator, or the All that Is. Any description we could come up with would be woefully inadequate because it could only be a comparison to something the author(s) of the Adam and Eve account could relate to.

For example, we are told that God is All-Good, that Heaven is perfect because that is where God is, and that the Garden of Eden was perfect. However, the accounts also relate that there was trouble in Heaven and in the Garden of Eden. They relate that everything the God-Creator created had problems—not just small insignificant problems but big, massive problems. There was a mutiny in Heaven led by Satan where one-third of the host of angels—probably innumerable beyond our imagination—sided with Satan and rebelled against God-Creator. And the perfect place on earth, created by the God-Creator Himself, was the origin of a negative force called *sin*. Thus, these are examples of what might be described as negative aspects of God-Creator.

Because of Adam and Eve, sin is said to have suddenly sprung into the world without any other explanation. Per the account, they committed a *particular sin*, but they did not create *sin itself* or the *possibility of sin*. The possibility of sin had to exist before they could commit a particular sin. So where did the possibility of sin come from? It could not have come from Adam and Eve. In our world, the possibility of something must exist before a particular thing can exist.

A possibility can be thought of as an undefined energy with the potential to be defined in a particular way.

Men and women are blessed with the ability to define (mold) that potential. In this, they are creators.

Undefined energy has a positive (+) pole and a negative (-) pole.

Thus, as the creators they are, men and women mold and shape the undefined energy.

The molding or shaping of the potential can lean towards the positive (+) pole or the negative (-) pole.

Molding or shaping the potential that affects others necessarily has a moral component. Thus, such molding or shaping of the potential may therefore be considered "Good" (+) or "Not Good" and "Evil" (-).

Per the accounts handed down to us, we think of God-Creator as All Good with nothing negative. Maybe that explanation is incomplete. Perhaps it's like thinking of a perfect thing like a battery with only one pole, the positive (+) pole but no negative (-) pole. But, you say, that couldn't exist. Without the negative pole, it wouldn't be a battery. There would be no flow of energy from one pole to the other. All of creation, at least as far as we can understand it, is like that—a combination of positive and negative, of what we might call "Good" and what we call "Not Good" where the energy flows from one pole to the other pole.

In the account of Adam and Eve, their disobedience is said to have ushered in "sin" as a result. But how was the possibility for that "sin" created? Where did it come from? Did someone or something create it and if so, who or what? Could it have come from God-Creator in some way which we do not understand? If God-Creator created the rules of the first man and woman and of the Garden of Eden, wouldn't those rules have to include the possibility and consequences of Adam and Eve not obeying

God-Creator? If so, wasn't the fall of Adam and Eve actually anticipated from all eternity?

If the negative consequence came from some source other than God-Creator, then you must posit a different creator, someone or something different from God-Creator.

We don't like the idea of something other than the God-Creator because we are taught that God-Creator created everything. This dichotomy gives us problems. If sin originated from some source other than God-Creator then we have to explain and deal with God-Creator not creating everything. Thus, there is more than one creator—there are at least two—God-Creator and some other creator! On the other hand, if we conclude that "Evil" and the possibility of sin is also created by God-Creator, along with everything else, then we have the problem of God-Creator not being All-Good (unless we conclude that the possibility of "evil" is also Good).

If you think about it, creation really is a messy business, at least the way we have experienced it. Creation means built-in problems and conflicts. If God-Creator had wanted only Himself to exist, then He wouldn't have done anything. He would be all there is—All-Good, perfection itself, and there would be no creation of anything else.

However, the way creation was "made" and unfolded, at least as far as we are concerned, conflict, issues, and problems were part and parcel of creation. Maybe there are some realms where creation is perfect, without built-in conflict and problems, but we know nothing of that.

Heaven itself must have been perfect, at least in the "beginning" because it was the "home" of the God-Creator. But consider what happened when He created the angels. Even in that most wonderful "place" where God-Creator "lived," a mighty mutiny and battle took place where it is said that one-third of the angels rebelled against God-Creator. Look what happened in the most perfect place on earth, the Garden of Eden. Satan, the leader of the mutiny and rebellion in Heaven, was allowed to enter and roam the Garden, was even invited into the Garden to cause another rebellion against God-Creator by Adam and Eve, and for which we are told, all mankind has suffered and is still suffering as a result.

Thus, we are told that everything God-Creator created had inherent issues, problems, unrest, and conflict. Notice that the inherent conflict always resulted in something different—a type of its own creation if you will.

Where there is conflict or a problem, things don't stay the same, rather, they change. The conflict or problem has to be addressed and solved, resolved or changed in some way. Thus, conflict or the problem itself is a type of birthplace and nursery where things are created. Everything is energy and energy is always in motion. Nothing stays the same but is always changing. Creation is like a built-in system of problem solution, problem solution.

It is said that the Scriptures are the inspired Word of God. Were the writers of the Genesis Scripture trying to tell us, *in code*, that creation itself is always moving and filled with inherent conflict and problems which become the birthplace of more creation—that conflict and problems must be addressed and resolved in some way thus creating something else?

That is a big and somewhat puzzling thought; at least that is how it must seem to us at first sight. Maybe there is an aspect of God-Creator whose essence is not inherent conflict and problems, which is perhaps concealed from us while we're on the earth. Perhaps that is the "place" or aspect of God-Creator that we go to after our earthly experience, where everything really is perfect and positive.

Here it may be helpful to think of God and God-Creator as two separate *aspects* of the One God. First there is God—complete unto Himself, perfection itself, not wanting or needing anything. Then, because God is God and All-Powerful, He "decides" to create by consubstantiating His Being into another Being thus creating another aspect of Himself, that being *God-Creator*. God-Creator then sets about creating the universe(s) and everything in it (them): angels, humans, animals, plants, etc. Perhaps God-Creator creates a universe(s) that is all positive (+) pole with no negative (-) pole, where there is not even the possibility of "Evil" or sin. We know nothing of that, nor do we have any experience of that. We can only imagine what it would be like: Heaven before the creation of Satan and the Garden of Eden before the "fall."

But we do know that God-Creator did create a universe, where we are, and which is based on both positive (+) poles and negative (-) poles. In this universe God-Creator manifests Himself in the infinite play of opposites. Thus, we can posit:

God: complete unto Himself

God-Creator: a consubstantiation of Himself which creates everything including our universe of positive (+) and negative (-)

Conflict, problems, and issues are our lot in life. From the moment we enter the earthly experience at conception and birth until we die and leave it, we are always having to deal with challenges, inherent conflicts, and problems dealing with ourselves, others, circumstances, and our surroundings. At every stage of life we are beset with them and are never free of them. Our life experience is filled with them. There is never a point or time in life which is free of them. Life is certainly a challenge all our life! As a youngster, I used to think that issues, problems, and challenges would stop sometime later in life when everything would be solved and resolved. Well, I realized they never end. It's the essence of creation itself as far as we know and experience it. Not all challenges, conflicts, and burdens are "heavy," but they're always present and we always have to deal with them throughout all stages of our lives.

We were taught that these lifelong and ever-changing problems, challenges, and disappointments were the direct result of Adam and Eve's Original Sin against God-Creator and that all mankind is being punished as a result of their sin. While I was in Catholic grade school, I remember thinking about what we had been taught—that all our difficulties and problems, like exams, having to study, learn difficult subjects, disease, disappointments, suffering, death, and all the other issues in life were the result of the sin of Adam and Eve. As I grew older and matured, that same thought was always in the back of my mind like an unseen computer program. It was something I didn't even have to think about as I went through life—jobs, education and higher education, relationships, etc. The specter of the fall of Adam and Eve was ever-present because it explained why things are as they are and why there are always problems and challenges in life. Furthermore, it was repeated simply as a given in life virtually everywhere—movies, TV, sports, media, news, books, magazine articles, and of course from the Church.

CHAPTER 12

THE SYNTHESIS

BASICALLY, THERE IS NO DICHOTOMY problem. There is only one God-Creator, and everything created by Him is "Good." There is no other creator of "Evil" or "Bad." However, God-Creator has also created the *potential* for men and women to create "Good" and "Not Good" or "Evil," i.e., things that gravitate more towards the negative pole of the *creation spectrum*. That's a core teaching in the Adam and Eve account. It's not a historical account of the first man and woman actually committing the first sin in defiance of God and for which all mankind is forever being punished.

It is very important to understand that all of salvation history does not fail just because there is no "Fall" of the first man and woman, Adam and Eve, and therefore no "Original Sin" as it has traditionally been taught and generally understood. The belief in a real Adam and Eve is not a requirement of faith. Christianity does not depend on the literal account of Adam and Eve being one-hundred percent true. Christianity does not rise or fall on the veracity of the Adam and Eve account. Furthermore:

1. The New Testament does not directly mention Adam and Eve but only mentions Adam peripherally. This notable silence, instead of emphasis, signals that it wasn't real.

2. Jesus does not directly mention Adam or Eve as personages which seems strange if He incarnated *because* of their fall.
3. You can still believe in the salvation work of Jesus and not believe in the literal account of Adam and Eve.
4. Salvation history remains intact and does not depend on the literal account of Adam and Eve.

Creation means that men and women have been given the *possibility* to create positive or negative, good or bad, and even evil things. This is how God-Creator made things. This is His creation, and we are living it and dealing with it. Admittedly, we cannot fathom or truly understand the depths of His decision. It simply is.

Also, men and women are created with the propensity to easily gravitate toward the negative possibilities. Again, we don't know why. It simply is. Thus, men and women can and do make wrong decisions, bad decisions, even evil decisions, and there are negative consequences. Therefore, we need to be "saved" from them and even ourselves. Through trial and error, we learn to make more positive decisions than negative decisions. Thus, in this whole process of trial and error, of learning how to create, we need mercy and love to keep going. It is not possible for us to just stop and leave the human race and not create any more. Creating is what we do all the time because our very essence is to create as does God-Creator and we are made in His image and likeness. God-Creator's answer to our need for mercy and to be saved from our bad and evil decisions is Jesus Christ. Again, we cannot fathom the depths of His decision about how to accomplish that, but we know that it simply is. Christianity is the ongoing reality of God's mercy and redemption in human history. Adam and Eve's fall are not needed for that. Christianity comes from Christ, not Adam or Adam and Eve. There's a reason it's called "Christianity" and not "Adamianity" or "Adamandeveianity."

Part of the rules of creation is that creation is messy business because it necessarily means that there will always be problems and issues which need to be dealt with (and sometimes created away) by defining or molding the undefined energy with our powers to create.

Rightly understood, the creation account of Adam and Eve is really a love story because it embraces the very essence of God-Creator, which is to create. God-Creator invites us to join our own creative powers with His to deal with, solve, and resolve the never-ending array of issues which continually arise in life. We don't have to face them alone because He is with us every step of the way. Thus, we join with God-Creator as Co-Creators molding and shaping the undefined potential energy into the healings and resolutions that we desire in our lives and in our world.

You don't have to live life very long to realize that everybody is always dealing with something—some difficulty, hardship, issue, conflict, etc. Remember, that's the story of creation. Creation means problems, difficulties, and issues. They existed even in the two perfect places we were told about by Scripture itself—Heaven and the Garden of Eden. If it happened in those perfect places, what makes us think we would be free of them? To be sure, we often have to deal with several problems and issues at the same time. In addition, there may be one issue in life which predominates. For some it's relationships, for others it's financial, and for still others it's health, etc. Whatever the issue or problem, whether it's predominant or not, it's a calling card or invitation from God-Creator to us. We don't have to face it alone. Rather, He's there to help us. We often forget that when we're dealing with an issue or problem, we arrive at the solution by co-creating with God-Creator. We can't do it alone; and by His own rules, He doesn't do it alone. Our part is to believe, be steadfast, do as much as we can, not worry, then let go and let God do His part. When Jesus solved issues and problems, He asked, "What do you want?" and "Do you believe?" The person participated in the healing action. It's hard to understand but issues and problems are God-Creator's invitation into deeper contact with Him. We always have problems, so we always have good reason to be in constant contact with Him.

CHAPTER 13

CONCLUSION

THE SCRIPTURAL ACCOUNT OF ADAM and Eve is an attempt by the writer(s) to explain, in some understandable way, the virtually unknowable concept of the aspect of God as Creator of *possibilities* for His creation of human men and women.

Fundamentally, human beings are created in the image and likeness of God in His creation aspect. That is to say, humans are basically creators, like their creator, God-Creator. He has made it possible for His human creation to create positive or negative, which are both "Good" in the sense that creation itself is "Good" and creating is "Good."

The scriptural writers had difficulty or did not know how to describe the aspect of God as opening the full breadth of creation (Good and Not Good) to humans without it sounding like God was both good and evil. So instead of trying to describe and have to try to defend God's creative nature as creating the *possibility* to create *Good and Evil*, it was easier to blame the Evil or "not good" aspect to a miscreant, a villain, a sinner, or Adam and Eve.

So, the reason our lives are filled with problems, conflicts, and challenges, is because God created it that way. The scriptural writers of antiquity and later couldn't come out and actually say that because it wouldn't be understood or accepted, and they would suffer the wrath of the ecclesiastical authority. It was much easier and palatable to lay the blame on one man and one woman in a colorful tapestry and perfect setting which they lost through sin thereby resulting in all men and women having to live under the shadow of their sin for all time.

Discoveries in science, technology, anthropology, and cosmology render the literal account of Adam and Eve more and more unlikely and many would say they debunk the account entirely. For example, it seems more and more likely that humans appeared on the scene at many places at the same general time rather than a single couple suddenly appearing alone in a single spot. Recent studies in several disciplines cast doubt on the very premise that modern humans have a single origin. On the contrary, there is growing evidence of interbreeding between human species across different regions. Bear in mind that Genesis 4 relates that after Cain killed his brother Abel, he was cursed by God such that the soil would not yield to him as a farmer anymore and he would have to be a homeless wanderer. Cain cried out to God that he feared others who found him would kill him. God then put a mark on Cain giving notice that anyone who killed him would suffer God's wrath and that seven lives would be taken in revenge. Cain left and lived in the land of Nod, east of Eden. Thus, the Bible itself acknowledges others who are not the offspring of Adam and Eve which leads to the inescapable conclusion that the account is flawed and not to be taken literally.

Also, the search for other beings in the cosmos has not gone unnoticed by the Church. The Vatican has an observatory in Italy and another one in Arizona manned by Jesuit astronomers! Pope Francis himself has spoken openly about the likelihood of beings in other worlds and even stated he would welcome them into the Church. Furthermore, he has stated that those other beings would not be tainted by Original Sin. As an aside, many years ago, my theology professor, who was an active theologian, taught us about a cutting-edge topic of the "Cosmic Christ" who would travel to other worlds saving those souls. Will we discover equivalent Adam and Eve accounts in other worlds?

All this goes to show that the account of Adam and Eve should not be thought of as static or fixed in "theological concrete" validating only the literal explanation. Rather, it beckons to be the subject of even more scrutiny and serious thought. The Pope, the Vatican, and theologians have been dealing with the big issue of where the Adam and Eve account, "Original Sin," and Christianity fit into the larger cosmic reality and where it fits into Christianity. There is a growing feeling that humanity is coming very close to being ready for bombshell-type discoveries that will impact our world and our beliefs forever. The belief in the existence of other beings in the cosmos is growing rapidly and evidenced by popular movies and programs such as *Ancient Aliens* and the *Star Trek* series which enjoy an increasing worldwide viewership.

Thus, there is an ever-growing virtual tidal wave of serious study and evidence, both ecclesiastical and secular, leading to the conclusion that we are not alone in the universe, that Adam and Eve were not the only created humans, that there were "others," perhaps human, perhaps not, and that a literal understanding of the creation account is flawed.

As noted in the beginning, important truths are often communicated and handed down to succeeding generations in stories, parables, and code using colorful descriptive tapestries to attract attention and to make them easily remembered. Just because the colorful tapestry is found to be imprecise doesn't mean the underlying truth is not correct.

At its core, the Adam and Eve account is a simple recognition that our life on earth is not easy or smooth and it was not intended to be that way. It is not the result of an "Original Sin" by a mythical or imaginary first couple. Rather, it's just the way things are; the way God-Creator made it. It is intended exactly as it is so that as God's creations, we know that we too can and must create all our lives. In doing so we solve and resolve the problems, issues, and conflicts we experience in life with God as the Ultimate Co-Creator. The problems and issues that are always with us are there for a reason. Jesus explains it very succinctly. In several instances Jesus is asked if a person's physical malady or death was caused by the person's sin or the sin of his father. He says "No," but that it is meant for the glory of God. Then the healing or miracle takes place. Thus, the malady or death was the magnet attracting God's healing presence which Jesus called forth. Are we being told, in coded form, that as co-creators, our destiny is to do the same as Jesus did and bring forth miracles and healings? Perhaps contacts with extraterrestrials are destined to assist us in that regard.

Is that the reason for so many difficulties and challenges in our lives—not to beat us down, but rather as gateways for God-Creator to enter our lives with healings and even miracles which we ourselves can call forth and participate in? Is the creation account not a tale of woe, of crime and punishment, but rather a call to co-create with God-Creator and bring forth healings and miracles? Are we now on the cusp of a new age of bringing miracles into our lives and discovering even more of God-Creator's magnificent creation with whom to relate? Might our future contacts with extraterrestrials usher in a new age of curing diseases and creating abundant energy wherever we want for our world?

God-Creator clearly likes problems, issues, and conflicts because He has created a fertile ground for them in this life. They provide a sure way for us to stay close to Him. So, when they arise, we should not be surprised, rather they should be expected. Most importantly, God-Creator knows that in this life we are practicing and learning how to create and sometimes we end up creating various levels of what is "Not Good" or "Not So Good." However, even that is "Good" because we learn how to create more "Good" than "Not Good." Also, God-Creator is always ready and willing to forgive and to help us deal with problems, issues, and challenges and to help us create more "Good." We will always have issues and problems in our life and God-Creator is always there helping us to solve and resolve them because He enjoys doing so. This is what He does. In this, He continues to create which is His essence and so do we because we are creators in His image and likeness. We are co-creators with God-Creator. Thus, God-Creator and His human creation become Co-Creators continually defining and molding the undefined energy to solve and resolve problems and limitations.

The writer(s) of the Adam and Eve account made it so implausible and God so conniving, backstabbing, and treacherous that it could *not* be taken literally. To do so you would have to believe that God is an ineffective coach and more evil than Satan. It's a colorful story whose important message, wrapped in pregnant brevity, has been taken literally and twisted into tortured and warped explanations of guilt and punishment which were certainly never intended and which make no spiritual or metaphysical sense. How could we have been so wrong for so long? What a travesty! On the shallow surface, it's a tragedy describing a vengeful god and horrible never-ending punishments for all mankind for all time. Delving deeper, it's a love story where a loving God-Creator invites all to "Come and create with me for you too are creators made in my image and likeness! Rejoice as together we create a new world now."

Now is the time to awake from our sleep of woe and punishment and take the reins of our God-given power to create more toward the positive (+) pole than the negative (-) pole.

Now is the time to remove the obfuscation and let the light of truth shine through to bring miracles into our lives as Jesus did. It's time!

NOTE FROM THE AUTHOR

AS I SAID AT THE outset, you are certainly free to make your own assessment of the ideas presented here. If you cringe at the very thought of them and are more comfortable with the traditional account of Adam and Eve, then I would simply say to stick with that. However, if you find that something here rings true for you, know that you are not alone. There is a growing chorus which simply feels that there is more to this account than the traditional explanations. They serve as a foundation, but a new generation feels the need to build on them and fill in the gaps to arrive at the greater truth which we are now able to understand and accept.

If you find that this message resonates with you at some level, either in agreement or disagreement, or you are simply curious about this topic and you have an open mind, realize that you are part of the expanding body of inquiring minds who know that big revelations to traditional understandings are coming and cannot be stopped or ignored. If you would like to be informed when other topics of this genre are addressed and ready for publication, often at the publisher's initial discounted prices, you may leave your email address here on my author page at https://gracepointpublishing.com.

Namaste.

FOR FURTHER REFERENCE

The Holy Bible, Revised Standard Version, Self-Pronouncing Edition. The World Publishing Company, 1962.
Catholic Church. 1997. *Catechism of the Catholic Church: Revised in accordance with the official Latin text promulgated by Pope John Paul II (2nd ed.).* Washington D.C.: United States Catholic Conference.
Consolmagno, Guy Br. SJ. 2015. *Welcome.* Home Page Vatican Observatory.
Consolmagno, Guy Br. SJ. 2019. *Guy Consolmagno, the Vatican's Chief Astronomer, On Science and Religion.* Vox.
Catholic News Service. 2011. *Catholic Church has evolving answer on reality of Adam and Eve.* U.S. Conference of Catholic Bishops.
Fox, Emmet. *Around the World With Emmet Fox: A Book of Daily Readings.* Harper Collins. 2010.
Fox News. 2015. *Vatican: It's OK for Catholics to Believe in Aliens.* Fox News.
Glatz, Carol. 2019. *Belief in aliens not so far out for some Catholics.* Catholic News Service.
Greenblatt, Stephen. 2018. *THE RISE AND FALL OF ADAM AND EVE.* W.W. Norton & Company.
Giangrave, Claire. 2017. *Could Catholicism handle the discovery of extraterrestrial live?* Faith and Culture Correspondent.
Hanger 1 The UFO Files. Amazon Prime. 2015.

Holmes, Jeremy Dr. 2012. *"Genesis 1-11 and Science."* Thomas Aquinas College.

Johnson, Elizabeth. 2018. *No one had to die for our sins.* U.S. Catholic.

Keim, Brandon. 2008. *Christian Theologians Prepare for Extraterrestrial Life.* ABC News.

Kosloski, Philip. 2017. *If aliens exist, can Catholics believe in them?* Spirituality.

Mazzola, Michael, Director. 2017. *Unacknowledged: An Expose of the World's Greatest Secret.* Amazon Prime.

Mazzola, Michael, Director. 2020. *Close Encounters of the Fifth Kind: Contact Has Begun.* Amazon Prime. Starring Steven Greer; Daniel Sheehan.

McIlmail, Edward Fr. LC. 2018. *"ASK A PRIEST: WHERE DID THOSE PEOPLE IN GENESIS 4 COME FROM?"* Regnum Christi Spirituality Center.

Mutual UFO Network (MUFON). 2021. mufon.com (accessed September 30, 2020).

Mulraney, Frances. 2015. *Vatican chief astronomer believes in UFOs and aliens.* IrishCentral.

Philips, Phil. 2018. *Mysterious Alignment of Ancient Sites.* Phil Philips.

Pullella, Philip. 2005. *Vatican scientist says belief in God and aliens is OK.* Reuters.

Holleman, Joseph. 2017. *Is there a relationship among all the pyramids in the world?* Quora.

Russell, Mary Doria, MA, PhD. 2014. *Jesuits in Space and in the Vatican.* Journal of the Catholic Health Association of the United States.

Sitchin, Zecharia. 2020. *ZECHARIA SITCHIN The Official Documentary.* The Sitchen Archives.

Vakoch, Douglas A. 2000. *Roman Catholic Views of Extraterrestrial Intelligence: Anticipating the Future by Examining the Past.* SETI Institute.

Von Däniken, Erich. *Chariots of the Gods.* Berkley, Reprint edition. 1984.

ABOUT THE AUTHOR

Ever thankful for his Catholic school background as well as his Jesuit University Undergraduate and Law School education, Mel Martinez feels well-grounded in the faith. His legal education and experience in the real world have taught him to instinctively go to the heart of a matter, identify key issues, separate fact from fiction, and extract the real meaning of things. Coupled with his lifelong interest in metaphysics and cosmology he perceives Scripture and matters of faith from a unique perspective. This affords him a way to decipher and interpret what is couched in symbolism, parables, code, and what he calls "Godspeak,"— the manner in which the Infinite chooses to communicate.

For more great books, please visit Empower Press online at
Books.GracePointPublishing.com

If you enjoyed reading *The Real Genesis Hidden in Plain Sight*
and purchased it through an online retailer, please return to the
site and write a review to help others find this book.

www.ingramcontent.com/pod-product-compliance
Lightning Source LLC
Chambersburg PA
CBHW070451050426
42451CB00015B/3431